The Book Your Evangelical Pastor Does Not Want You to Read

Religion Busters

Setting You at Liberty from Man-Made Doctrines Embrace Grace Plus Nothing

Don Keathley

Religion Busters

http://www.donkeathley.com/

God No Religion
All Rights Reserved.
https://www.godnoreligion.com/

Author: Don Keathley

Inspired writer, transcriber:
Natasha Trezebiatowski

Editor and Proofreading:
Jack Minor

Facebook: Don Keathley Ministries
YouTube: Don Keathley

Don Keathley Websites:
http://www.donkeathley.com/
https://www.gracepointnetwork.com/
http://globalgraceseminary.net/

The Scriptures are taken from the New King James Bible or otherwise listed. All quoted comments in the book are by Don Keathley or otherwise listed.

This book is transcribed from the Don Keathley YouTube teaching, Religion Busters, along with additional teaching.

Religion Busters and Hell's Illusion are the Don Keathley foundational teachings on God's grace, and unconditional love. Don's teachings in these two books will set you on your path to mind freedom. Moving you from out of the constraints of man-made religion, and into knowing God's grace and unconditional love for all humanity.

Don Keathley Religion Busters Series YouTube:

Religion Busters, 2-part series:

https://youtu.be/yEL2IQ24ptw

Hell's Illusion, Amazon in print and eBook:

https://www.amazon.com/dp/B08DF828H2/ref=mp_s_a_1_1?dchild=1&keywords=hells+illusion&qid=1595456486&sr=8-1

Hell's Illusion, 6-part YouTube series:

https://youtu.be/ILK_eem1Xi0?list=PLOzLQrpouifUrNvmCwN_qs9g1-3jfXZV3

http://www.hellsillusion.com/

Dedication

To all of my spiritual family, I wrote Religion Busters for you. I want to encourage you in making the quantum leap of grace and unconditional love, and for you to have the revelation of the finished work of the cross which leads you into mental freedom.

I know just how difficult and frightening the journey of moving out of the constraints of religion can be. It involves a major shift and adjustment and often a total undoing of doctrines that have become deeply embedded in us over decades.

It is your time now to sit back and relax. Enjoy the journey God is about to take you on as I go through some of the common mindset traps that may still have you in bondage. I will unravel some of the man-made religious roadblocks that have held you back and stopped you from leading the full abundant life that Jesus personally designed for you, without any effort.

It is called the gift of grace, so enjoy unwrapping this gift that will keep on giving all the way into eternity.

God Bless you,

Don Keathley

Hell's Illusion - Don Keathley

"The realization that we believe we have to serve God out of fear will reveal more about the truth that lies within our hearts. Are we a Christian because we love God? Or are we a Christian because someone put the hell gun to our head, so we better do it, or else?

We think that saying a few religious confessional words will prevent us from forever residing in a place called hell. We confess Scriptures and do many great things for God because we believe it will please him, thereby keeping us out of hell. The church puts us in a position where it controls us, and this control does not have its root in love. The freedom to love is what brings forth a heartfelt change, not from out of fear."

Hell's Illusion – Exposing the Myth of Hell

https://www.amazon.com/dp/B08DF828H2/ref=mp_s_a_1_1?dchild=1&keywords=hells+illusion&qid=1595456486&sr=8-1

Hell's Illusion Testimonials

Brenda Weidenhammer

"Life changing book for me! Unbelieving in hell has removed so many fears for me. I highly recommend the book or the series by Don Keathley. I so appreciate that wonderful man who has been, and continues to be, very instrumental in my Jesus walk. Thank you so much, Don Keathley."

Natasha Trezebiatowski

https://www.godnoreligion.com/

"I wholeheartedly want to thank Don Keathley who is a tremendous grace teacher and mentor in my own personal journey with the Father. Don's teachings continue to bring me refreshing revelation, and when I hear Don teach, it's like hearing my Father speak directly to my spirit with His unconditional love. I encourage you to read Don Keathley's book *Hell's Illusion* which reveals all the true correct Greek words Jesus spoke regarding hell. It will transform your thinking and you will be released from a fear driven mind-set which only seeks to keep you in torment. This whole mythological place called hell which the church still persists in teaching, has dominated and controlled people for far too long. It is time to set yourself free from false fears and being held under religious control and embrace our Fathers pure heart and purpose; His all-consuming unconditional fire of love for all of humanity."

Priscilla Eastern Canada

"Taking away the belief in Hell, has helped me fearlessly pursue truth. A little over a year ago, my friend said that if I studied the Greek, I would know that Hell didn't exist. I was afraid to check into it because of the loss of friendship and possibly going to Hell. Lol. It seemed like a slippery slope. A few months later, I asked her for some information, and she sent the links to "Hell's Illusion." I cannot even express the freedom that came from those teachings. It never really sat well with me that a loving God would torture people with an everlasting punishment. I just swallowed the Kool-Aid with everyone around me."

"Thank you, Don Keathley, for what you do!! I am a life changed."

Michelle Townsend

"From the time I was a little girl, I was told that Hell existed. I was warned that I could go there for not praying a prayer of salvation, so I prayed the prayer. I was told that I could grow lukewarm and still go to Hell, so I started getting worried every night that I wasn't as close to God as I should be, and I would go to my parents and cry because I was so afraid. They would create a new prayer and pray it with me, but I still was uncertain about my eternal destination. This went on for several years, and I even had nightmares about Hell. I was so tormented that even as an adult, I had a few breakdowns where I was worried that I was going to go to Hell for not reading my Bible enough. As I've since started learning about grace and that it's not about my efforts, but Christ's to save me, the doctrine of Hell again surfaced. But this time, something just didn't add up, though I didn't have much information. Pastor Don's series on "Hell's Illusion" is like nothing I've ever heard before! It literally was the first time I had heard what the words (translated as Hell) actually mean! Don is very courageous to tackle such a hot and heavy issue. I, like many others, am relieved to know what these words really mean. It's a big sigh of relief to know the truth now!"

Jim Wright

"I was struggling with Hell being real or not. I was attending church at the time and had heard a couple of views of Hell not being real. I went to my Pastor and told him what I had heard and that I had been studying it and if it was or wasn't true. He gave me a two-hour lecture without listening to a single thing I said. He had me almost convinced that it was. A couple of days later, I stumbled upon Don's "Hell's Illusion" teachings. I listened to all of them twice, and it sent me into revelation and a history study. I got into Greek and Hebrew translations and found my truth of Hell not being a real place. This teaching changed me, and it changed how I read and study Scripture. It was a necessary piece of the puzzle in the transformation for me to move into Sonship."

About Religion Busters

Our Father is doing an incredible work today, and it's a tsunami of his love, grace, and mercy. He is passionately pursuing you, and his love is an all-consuming refining fire that will transform and fill you with joy, peace, and prosperity in every area of your life. The only thing stopping you from receiving your full inheritance is the fortress in your mind created by religion in its efforts to control you and stop the eternal flow in your life.

Today, there is a mass movement of multitudes coming out of religious bondage into the Father's heart of grace and unfailing love. We now recognize the words of Jesus in John 8:32, ***"And you shall know the truth, and the truth shall make you free."***

I want to welcome you as a family member to my weekly teaching on YouTube at the Digital Cathedral and on Facebook at Don Keathley Ministries. Many people who journeyed with me have realized that religion is not something that they really desire to be a part of, and they are now stepping away from it because, in their spirit, it no longer resonates.

It is time to bust this false lie of religion wide open and set all people free from human-made false, fear-driven doctrines, and lead you to the freedom from sin-consciousness that religion has infected and bound within your mind through their relentless, repetitive lies.

You are about to embark on a wild ride through the horror of what religious lies have done to hold you back from the truth in his grace and unconditional love. As you journey through this book, the tremendous freeing revelation will bring you out of the dark religious dungeon which has imprisoned your mind and lead you to his marvelous light, and his unfailing and empowering unconditional love. I encourage you to read this book and take a step forward towards your mental freedom, becoming secure in the knowledge that you are no longer trapped in a revulsion of unpardonable sin, as religion would like you to believe. It is time to take a hold of your freedom and live life removed from the struggles and anxieties that consume people in this world through the corruption of lies.

Religion Busters will break you free from human-made theology built on straw, with no solid rock foundation or life-giving support. I'm busting open this idea of human separation from the Spirit of God within you through sin or having an Adamic nature, and that we are born totally depraved. I'm bringing religion down so you can see we're talking about a matter of identity and the finished work of the cross. It is all finished, and you do not need to do anything to obtain what Christ has already done for you. His only request is that you rest in him.

The Kingdom of God is within you and Christ has always been with you, just waiting for you to receive your eternal riches. Dominating religious forces have prevented you from entering into his divine supper that he has already prepared for you.

The Spirit of Truth is going to triumph in the end over any religious denominations because they have no foundation where people can live and breathe easy. The voice of God is going to really start trumpeting through your spirit as you embrace grace and deconstruct your religious idols. No longer will you remain in bondage, and under the pressures of society with its constant struggle to perform for God, trying to meet impossible standards. God's amazing pure love has spoken to you; you've heard him, and you no longer desire to be confined to a human-made religious prison.

We are not tied to religion; we are secure in our spirit and mind in the Lord Jesus Christ who is within us and hearing him directly for our individual lives. We're coming into a new season; it's universal, and it is happening in every corner of the earth. I want to make sure we are not bringing any baggage of institutional religion along with us; and the reason for this book is to ensure we bust open the common tempting mind traps that attempt to deter us from truth through religious lies. The more we can cut off and understand how religion ensnares us the freer we become. Religion is the thing that keeps you unsure and off-balance, preventing you from feeling secure while you are always trying to attain.

At some point, we have all come under some form of religion, even Christian religion with its toxic mixture of Old Testament rules along with a blend of New Testament grace. You will read why we no longer follow any of the traditions in the Old Testament, which Jesus Christ rendered obsolete. We live our life in Christ Jesus, which is the Kingdom of God here now within you. Everything you need for your life is available not through rituals, but rather is manifested from out of your relationship with him.

This book is the start of it all, and this is where you will discover some new insights and revelations that perhaps you have never had before. Your old thought patterns will be wiped away, never to come back again and you will experience freedom in Christ as you were always designed to do. Our mindsets are everything, and this is why you conduct yourself in the manner you do, and every action you take has come through your thought pattern. For far too long, people have misinterpreted what the Bible means. It's been lost in the translation. Many of us have just assumed what things mean by listening to other people rather than searching it out for ourselves and hearing from his Spirit within. This book will unravel twisted religious Scriptures and present the message of grace and the finished work of the cross.

You're about to start your detox and begin moving from out of the clutches and shackles of human-made rules, laws, regulations, and constraints. You will feel freedom like you have never felt before, and it all begins with grace embodied in a person, Jesus Christ.

Yep, that's right, it's all finished! It's now your time to breathe, relax, and receive. No longer will anything or anyone have control over you, and from this point forward it's a new walk where you are walking with God and hearing from him yourself through love, purpose, and passion in his Spirit that is within you.

After reading this book, I hope you never again see yourself as being not even one degree separated from God, your Father, who unconditionally loves you. You will find mental freedom, clarity, and peace of mind, and this is the liberty that God planned for you since before the foundation of the world.

It's time to grab that big old Bible from your coffee table, dust it off and take a journey with me as we go through some religious lies and then reap the everlasting truth from the living word who is Christ in you the hope of glory.

Introduction to Religion Busters

Do you still wrestle with this idea of whether or not you are saved? Are you afraid you might be lost? How can you be certain that you are saved? I mean, surely you need to do certain things if you want to get your name written in God's good book and remain in his good graces, right? Wrong! In this book, I will bust open the perception woven into us by our religious upbringing which says we were born with our life spiritually separated from God, which is not true.

When I talk about religion, I am not referring to individual people. I don't want you to feel like I'm putting any person down; that is not the purpose of my teachings. I understand there are millions of great sincere people in the world, and I have many friends who remain trapped in religion's clutches.

Today, many people have become institutionalized into believing the doctrines of false human-made systems through teachers who have selected and cherry-picked specific Scriptures to control people because they believe in an angry and judgmental God. Whatever you believe you will demonstrate in your life, and many teachers of the law have been taking the Scriptures and twisting them into heartless orders that serve only to produce robotic cold people who perform righteous acts outwardly in their attempt to be made acceptable before God.

If you want the blessings of health and prosperity, they have the answer for how to obtain your desire through behavior modification. The only issue with their religious theory is your heart. If your heart believes a certain way, then no matter how much you try to make yourself behave outwardly according to specific rules, it will not work. Your heart will always direct your mind, and your mind will go on to direct your actions. No matter how hard you try to perfect yourself, you can never be perfect. If you are going to be obedient to the law then you need to be obedient to the entire law, not just one part of the law; and this is impossible. Jesus fulfilled the law, period.

Religion Busters will eliminate your religious consciousness and all the myths and lies you may still be clinging onto, some of which perhaps you haven't yet realized. Many of us have had 30+ years of soaking up what religion has fed us week after week, year after year. This has become so prevalent and saturated us that it has now become deeply ingrained within us. It has been said that if you hear a lie often enough, you will eventually believe it as the truth. I've certainly had this happen to me in my life through years of religious believing, so I can relate to and understand this whole religious façade.

The Bible is not God's word, no matter what we have all been taught; it is a book that was written by people who were inspired by God. Jesus Christ said in John 5:39, ***"You search the Scriptures, for in them you think you have eternal life, and these are they which testify of Me."*** He is God's living word, and when we read Scripture, we are made alive and receive revelation through him, not mere words. He is the One who sheds light on the words we read. In Hebrews 4:12 it states that he is the One who is alive and active, sharper than any double-edged sword. When we read, his Spirit within us will supercharge our spirit, causing it to penetrate even to dividing of soul and spirit, joints and marrow. Once there, what we receive will then judge our thoughts and the attitudes of our hearts.

The word religion comes from the Latin word *"Religio,"* and the definition is; *an obligation by humans to their God.* In other words, something is expected and required from humans for them to give to God in return for God's peace, God's blessing, and God's prosperity. I think we can say religion is the consummate trade-off, and it's an obligation that we sense we have to give something to God in order for God to bless us back.

In religion, God looks at us and says, *"I demand your allegiance, and I demand your worship, I demand that you recognize Me, I need something from you, and I want you to be obligated to Me. If I receive that worship, that obligation, that commitment from you, then I will bless you back and prosper you."*

Depending on the God you worship, these demands can be anything from throwing a virgin into the volcano, praying the magic prayer, dedicating your life to him; it can be all kinds of things. What is expected from people under religious control, no matter what your religious label is, will always require rituals and sacrifices to varying degrees.

If you look a little bit deeper into the word *religio*, it comes from two words, the word *re*, which is the prefix meaning to return to. Anytime you return to something, you take it back. So, the prefix *re* means simply to return, and *legion* means to bind. What religion is, in its purest sense is a return to bondage. It's this formal *religio* of bondage that Jesus completely destroyed. He did not come to set up another *religio.* He did not come to establish the Baptist religion, he didn't come to establish the Catholic religion, he didn't come to establish any religion. He came to do away with religion altogether and bring all of humanity to a knowledge of him personally.

The word Busters in the title of this book comes from *"Busted,"* which was a new term for me. I learned this word from my grandson. It's a slang term that means your wrongdoing has been brought to light! The wrong has been uncovered. You've been discovered and called out, and you didn't get away with it!

I always thought that busted only meant something was broken, and this definition certainly applies because religion is a broken, failed system. Religion has two starting points, and here is where we have a problem with authentic identity. The first one is the fall of mankind, and Adam is where the church generally starts the story. If not there, they begin it at the cross. Both begin with the idea of separation, and if the story for you begins in Adam, then you're automatically spiritually separated, and if it begins at the cross, we have a separation that Jesus fulfilled. Religion has its roots in control, and this control has its origins deep within fear, and anyone seeking to control you will be serving their own judgmental angry God that has been totally fabricated in their mind. Fear is the breeding ground for captivity, and so long as you live with some form of fear, you will remain a hostage to it.

Each chapter will symbolize some of the common traps religion has used to keep the body of Christ in bondage, along with the message of freedom through the finished work of the cross; grace and unconditional love. We will begin by uncovering what religion is and what it has done to countless people's minds across the world over the many years since its origin. The apostle Paul is our New Testament theologian educator who brought us the grace message, not through any seminary institutions nor through any human. He had a direct revelation from God. We will take a close look at his teachings, particularly through the book of Galatians where he was grieved to hear people had mixed pure grace with legalism. I will highlight some of the Scriptures through the Old Testament, and the words Jesus spoke to the religious people in his time to bring down the human-made establishment.

The journey concludes with some powerful encouragement for you to walk out your life daily through his grace and unconditional love that is all encased in the One Spirit within you. Grace is the person of Christ Jesus and living out your life through having daily conversations with him. He alone is the living word of God who speaks directly to you and will inspire the steps that you take.

Religion Busters is part of my foundation series from moving out of religion and into a relationship with Christ. I recommend you read my book, *"Hell's Illusion"* and gain a mind assurance over the false deception that hell exists. Hell is a myth created by religious people to govern you. The hell doctrine is yet another form of Scripture that is perverse and a complete lie. I have revealed all the correct original Greek words Jesus spoke when he uses the word hell. To find out more, you can purchase your copy at Amazon:

https://www.amazon.com.au/Hells-Illusion-Don-Keathley-ebook/dp/B08DF828H2

Or listen to the YouTube six-part teaching series: https://youtu.be/ILK_eem1Xi0

These are great introductory truths and a starting point for you to be released from religion and into a relational revelation through our Abba Father, and his Son Christ, who is the living Spirit within you. Once you enter into a relationship in his unconditional love, you're automatically going to have a heartfelt change enter your mind. You will not need to look at any written laws because you will know his heart for you in everything you do as you walk through life together in union.

This book presents an Almighty *"Kaboom"* of revelation that will downpour Christ's power and his all-consuming fire of passionate love for you within your heart. The floodlight is on, and your one key to autonomy is to know him, and then your mind will be focused on living your life on earth just as it is in heaven. I always say, don't take my words as the gospel truth. After reading this book, go and do your own research, and investigate things. Sit with God, and meditate on the Truth, and allow the Spirit of Truth to speak to you. You have the Christ Spirit, and he alone will speak and bear witness within you.

You're no longer being robbed blind by the smooth criminal of religion any longer. It is time to bust free from the chains of darkness, ripping off the religious veil. It is time to tell religion that it's been caught and can no longer get away with damaging and demanding human-made lies that have caused endless fear, stripping you of your true identity in the Father. Religion is history, and once you read this book, you will never again accept anything less than your full inheritance, and to know who you are in him.

You will shut the door firmly on human-made doctrines, bolt them up, and never will they open again!

"I want to make it very clear to you my friends that the message I proclaim is not mere speculation or the product of philosophical or religious debate. This is not my own invention, neither was I spoon-fed by human tuitions, my source of reference is the unveiling mystery of Christ in me. God's eternal love dream separated me for my mother's womb; his grace became my identity. It pleased the Father to reveal his Son in me in order that I may proclaim him in the nations!" Galatians 1:11-12, 1:15-16 Mirror Bible

Contents

Chapter 1

~The Good News~

"Salvation is not something to be attained; it is something you realize as the finished fact of the reality of Jesus' death and resurrection for all humans."
Don Keathley

God's grace and unconditional love is beginning to surface to the forefront of people's consciousnesses. After years of being held in religious human-made systems, we are now breaking free. I do believe the majority of religious people are sincere and want to please God, and at some point in each of our lives, we too have been under its constraints. Religion is humanity's effort to self-generate an acceptance and entry to God through our efforts, which can be relentlessly exhausting for our mind and body.

Every day, multitudes of people are having the revelation of Christ within through the finished work of the cross, and they are now enjoying their newfound freedom in him through grace and unconditional love. If, in this moment, you are not content nor can you feel the freedom from bondage and anxieties that religion has been pouring out on you, then it's now time to eliminate the frustrations of relying on yourself. If you feel the pressure of a heavy load in your mind, keep pressing into Christ because he will show you himself and uproot any religious and self-orientated blocks. The Father's immeasurable love is for all people, including those who do not believe or have had a revelation of Christ in them, because he is the Savior and creator of all humanity. He wants everyone to enjoy an abundant life in him, right now and onto all eternity. God will never stop pursuing every human until every knee shall bow to the Lord Jesus Christ.

You might be asking yourself, *"Did I just read, right? Did Don Keathley just say that everyone is already saved and in Christ?"* Yes, that is exactly what I am saying. Every human has God's Spirit within, as we read in Genesis 1:26. God said, ***"Let us make man in our image, according to our likeness."*** We are all born from God. No man has entered the world through any means, other than God breathing life into them. The atonement was collective. It was for every human, and everyone needs to have that revelation revealed of who they are in Christ. In 2 Corinthians 5:15, Paul says, ***"And he died for all, that those who live should live no longer for themselves, but for him who died for them and rose again."*** In this Scripture, we understand that there is nothing you can do in any of your efforts to die with Christ. He died for all of humanity, and we are raised in him, as we read in 2

Timothy 2:11. ***"This is a faithful saying: For if we died with him, we shall also live with him."*** Christ has died for every human, and this means we have already died! If you were ever wondering about death, you don't need to anymore because you already experienced it, and it was pain-free and fear-free because Christ did it for you, as you. You live in all eternity with your Father right now through the indwelling of his Spirit in yours, and you are seated in the heavenly realm. Just focus your mind to him. It is not the flesh, meaning your body and soulish thought realm, that gives you your life. It is your spirit that is your very being, and it is fully connected to the Father as we read in John 6:63. ***"It is the Spirit who gives life, the flesh profits nothing, the words that I speak to you are spirit, and they are life."*** In just these two Scriptures alone we read what Paul said to Timothy, that if we died with him, we also live with him. We played no part in God's unconditional love for us; and becoming one with Christ had nothing to do with any of your bad or good behaviors. He took all of humanity into himself, and we have been simulated into his life. In John 1:9 (paraphrased), he says, ***"Jesus is the light that lights every man that comes in the world."*** Jesus is the light that illuminates *every human* who comes into the world, it is through our revelation that we know the truth. Your Salvation is sealed, and all of humanity from past, present, to future, all have the Spirit of Christ. Indeed, it is great news that every promise is yes because we have our guarantee in him, and everything consists in him. ***"For all the promises of God in him are Yes, and in him Amen, to the glory of God through us." (2 Corinthians 1:20)***

It is God who directs us to know that we are in Christ and that he is our assurance of eternal life. Since we are all sealed from before the foundation of the world, are we going to believe that the creator of the world as a whole, who is omniscient and omnipotent, is going to leave everything up to us and our choice? He is not leaving anything up to us at all, he has done it all himself, and he made a covenant with himself for our sake, as we read in Ephesians 1:4. ***"Just as he chose us in him before the foundation of the world, that we should be holy and without blame before him in love."*** Paul teaches us through the Spirit of revelation in 2 Corinthians 1:21-22 that everything has already been fulfilled for you, which you know because you have the Holy Spirit. ***"Now he who establishes us with you in Christ and has anointed us is God, who also has sealed us and given us the Spirit in our hearts as a guarantee."***

God has always been calling you to himself, to look within; and the day your heart agreed with God's heart was the day you genuinely confessed from an overflowing heart of love that Jesus is Lord of your life. We can certainly confess Scripture without having the revelation of his truth, however, confessing Scripture does not *"Save you"* as religion teaches. Jesus Christ is the One who has already saved you since the world began.

In Galatians 2:20, Paul is talking about being crucified with Christ, but not only about himself. He is speaking to every person and letting them know that they are now no longer dependent upon themselves because they have the complete power and victory of life in Christ. Just as Paul made this statement about himself, you too can joyfully confess this over yourself. ***"I have been crucified with Christ; it is no longer I who live, but Christ lives in me, and the life which I now live in the flesh I live by faith in the Son of God, who loved me and gave himself for me."*** We have been totally identified with Christ in his crucifixion. And then in Ephesians 2:6, we read, ***"And raised us up together, and made us sit together in the heavenly places in Christ Jesus."*** Not only were we crucified with Christ, he has raised us up together and made us sit with him in the heavenly places. What was it that you did exactly? Nothing! Christ did it all for you, and there was nothing for you to do but rest in him, and that is the good news. In fact, it is the best news! We are included in him at all times, no matter what we do in life. Whether or not we believe in him has nothing to do with what he has done for all of humanity. God's light will illuminate and shine right through even the hardest person. And once they know pure, authentic love they cannot turn back to darkness. The power of his love will supersede any demands and hostility regimented within the mind.

"Religion will always use the Bible to prove the Bible. The Spirit of Truth whom Jesus sent to lead and teach you will speak to you directly, and the unconditional love of the Father will always be the lens he reveals through."

As believers in Christ who have the revelation of his all-consuming love, we get the amazing opportunity to share our life with our Father now, and to know the right way to live and enjoy life through a relationship with him. We get to experience our life in all abundances through his promises, and this gives us a more significant advantage as we walk in the Kingdom of God and eat from the tree of life. People who chose not to believe or have not had the revelation of Christ miss out on a beautiful union with him now. However, that can change at any time, and God will never stop pursuing people right through all of eternity to know him. We have a present tense ongoing growth and grace experience that never ends. He continues to strengthen that seal which goes on within us by continued revelation and awakening. In 1 Timothy 4:10, Paul says that Jesus is the Savior of all men, and especially, but not exclusively, to those that believe. Believing is a response, and it gets grander and deeper with each revelation as we journey with God throughout our life. We feel a superior safety and continued strength the more we live from knowing his unconditional love for us. We are to work out our Salvation and it is God who works in us both to will and to do of his good pleasure. (Philippians 2:12-13) We live our lives from out of him and it is up to us individually to work out all that he has deposited within us. God has worked his good pleasure in us, and then we are to work out our Salvation which is bringing, from out of our spirit being, all that he has deposited into us. We must not lose sight of what God has done through Christ for our Salvation, redemption, and reconciliation of the entire cosmos. Religion will reduce it down to a transaction deal, where you have done your part and God must now do his part! Jesus Christ made a covenant that could not be broken. He made the covenant with the Father through his death, burial, and resurrection, and he included you in it every step of the way. It is time that we let go of all the religious hocus pocus that you have been raised to believe and were taught. You no longer need to jump through hoops and do many religious acts to be accepted into God. All you do now is rest.

David realized that no matter what he did, God was always with him and this is the very same vision that we must come to realize. He said, ***"Where can I go from your Spirit? Or where can I flee from your presence? If I ascend into heaven, you are there, if I make my bed in***

hell, behold, you are there, If I take the wings of the morning and dwell in the uttermost parts of the sea, even there your hand shall lead me, and your right hand shall hold me." (Psalm 139:7)

David gives us a brilliant insight into the Omnipresence of God. He says there's no place that you can run from God, though you may try. But guess what? You can't hide from God! David is explaining to us that God's presence, his love, and his goodness are totally inescapable, and no matter what you do, you cannot outrun God's love he has for you.

Wherever you find yourself in life right now, the good news is that God is with you, and you can't escape the promises that he has for you. Even if you don't really know him, David tells us that his right hand is still upholding you. Religious systems are the launchpad for virtually every belief that has woven its way into the church over the last 2,000 years. It is considered pure Orthodox teaching and beyond the realm of questioning, and we dare not query what we are taught. We just accepted what they fed us week after week, never looking into it for ourselves. We've tried to work it out religiously in some way through many different formulas and methods. We didn't set out to intentionally fall into the trap of religious practices; it was bestowed upon us, and we believed the lie they fed us that we are born in sin. Hearing this repeatedly and believing in the falsehood that we are separated from our Father's will has negatively impact our lives through how we see him and how he sees us. It is a debilitating mind game of deceits to believe we are all outcasts in God's eyes, and only if we do what religion deems as the right thing to do can we be acceptable to him. We are persuaded into a fear-based doctrine, and we keep going back to the church to hear from the pastor or priest to give us a sense of security. Interestingly, religion tells us that God creates all humans, yet they teach a very contradictory doctrine of separation that we are born in Adam! They teach us that we are created in Adam's image and likeness, and we are sinners; therefore, we must perform outward good works if we are to be acceptable to God.

We know through the Spirit of Truth and Scripture that he placed his likeness and image in all humanity, and therefore we are created with his DNA through what Christ has finished and completed for us. Religion tells us that we are now children of the devil because of Adam's sin. In essence, this supposed evil spiritual being has given life to all people born into the earth with his nature and DNA! That really does sounds crazy, yet even I, at one point, fell victim to this lie. We just assumed that we were born sinners, depraved, born with an Adamic nature, and we are born separated from God, therefore we must *do* something to be acceptable to God; otherwise, we go to hell for all eternity. Religion will control your mind, and fear can produce many unhealthy results for yourself and your family, and all the people you come in contact with daily. Religion kills your spirit and soul that hungers for God as they feed you through anxiety, which will manifest itself into all kinds of disturbing thoughts that then come into your reality.

There are so many different religions from the Catholic church, the Presbyterian, the Baptist, and even the modern Pentecostal Christian faiths, and they all have their roots in fear; do this to please God or else. They don't share with you the truth of Scripture or the Father's loving heart. They want you to stay in a system that has been tested repeatedly through the years to produce money for them. They are not going to allow people the opportunity to really be free when it's going to cost them countless dollars, and they may have to forfeit their titles. However, I believe the majority of religious teachers are strongly fixed in what they believe to be true. It is for this reason that only Christ can help them to see true freedom. There are still countless pastors who love the Lord yet remain under the bondage of control, and they are not aware of it because religion is such a strong influence. We entered these institutions going on what we knew at the time, until we figured out that it was wrong.

Adam certainly thought in his mind that he was separated from God, and we know this by his actions. In Genesis 3:8, we read that Adam was trying to hide from God, and we can relate to wanting to hide when we do things out of a wrong belief that is hidden inside us. We develop mind separation through the fear doctrine we had been taught, instead of going directly to God and working out our Salvation. Adam thought God was angry with him, yet God's response was not one of separation. God responded and said in Genesis 3:9-11 (paraphrased), ***"Why are you hiding from Me Adam? And who told you that you were naked?"*** We automatically respond the same way Adam did, thinking we need to hide from God through our religious mindset. We have all kinds of guilts and condemnations that rise within us due to all the laws, rules, and regulations we've heard that we failed to keep when we signed on the dotted line and joined that church. This guilt produces all kinds of reactions and actions within us, and we don't go to church, we don't pray, we don't fellowship, and we won't read our Bibles or any materials, we just keep ourselves separated and cut off from God. This was the great lie brought in by religion, which misinterpreted what happened to Adam.

The fact is, Adam was working out in his own mind things that were not grounded in truth. He believed a lie, an illusion which opened the door for all men to walk in. Adam believed in himself. In his mind, he walked away from God through his actions and what he did through mind separation, which demonstrated to people that they too could walk alone. We now have the propensity to do the same through what we have learned in our family and how others walked before us, which all originated from Adam's rebellion. He showed all of humanity they could pull away and be their own god, where the ego will take hold of a person, which is eating from the tree of knowledge of good and evil. (Genesis 2:17)

The tree of knowledge of good and evil is trying to get your nutrition through written laws and rules. It is a system whereby you are trying in your own strength to learn and do what is right and acceptable before God. However, when you are in a relationship with God through unconditional love and grace, you will naturally do and live out your life doing what is right and beneficial. God removes your cold heart and puts his heart inside of you, then you automatically have no need for written laws to tell you what is right and wrong. And through his love, you have no fear. If at any time you are tempted to do something that you really know is not right, that is the time to talk with your Father and open up a conversation with him about your desires, even if they are not right because he will shed light on what is right. Once you see the truth on the topic, it will break down and dissolve any wrong tempting thoughts that are not beneficial for you and other people. He only wants what is best for you, so you are never going to miss out on anything. All the prosperity, which includes health, is all yours and he wants you to receive it from him.

When you let go of rules and your way being the right way and then come to that perfect freedom of surrender and fall into his love for you, everything you do will be easy. There is no burden, your heart is his heart, and your desires are his desires. In James 1:4 we read that you will lack nothing if you keep walking with God and be patient with yourself, trust him, and be open to working out your Salvation with him. And as you do, you will find that you will have everything you desire.

"But let patience have its perfect work, that you may be perfect and complete, lacking nothing."
James 1:4

We are not separated from God by sin. It is not written in Scripture anywhere that the inspired writers ever thought that way. Here is the key to what James is explaining to us as he continues in James 1:14-15. ***"But each one is tempted when he is drawn away by his own desires and enticed. Then when desire has conceived, it gives birth to sin, and sin when its full-grown, brings forth death."*** When we do wrong things, we are pulled away because of our own natural inclinations that have nothing at all to do with having the nature of Adam. The ego wants things for selfish reasons, and we can self-talk ourselves into justifying why we followed through with our temptations. God is our origination who we always reside in, and he speaks to us daily. He is encouraging us, but we do not always want to hear him, which can then lead us to walk in error.

Sin is being separated from God in your mind, and anytime you are disconnected from God and are not walking with him, it will open that same door as Adam. We need to separate Adam out of this, and just as James said in 1:4-5, we need to take responsibility for where our minds are going. We have scapegoated Adam long enough and blamed him for far too long. Even if he did open that door of the tree of good and evil, we have our own minds and we can make our own choice with God or against God. You need to grasp that you can have an easy burden-free life through a relationship with God, talking to him as you connect to him daily in union and unconditional love. You do have a choice which way you want your life to be influenced. We do not want to travel down that same rocky road Adam traveled on, and anyone who went along the same route in the Bible fell into the same disconnected consequences with God. They had dilemma after dilemma when all they had to do was step back and go to God and seek him for their life. I'm not sure why we think that we know better, and can produce a better outcome than what God gives us, because history, through the Bible, shows us that we will lose every time we continue down on our own path.

Religion says you have messed up, and now you cannot go to your Father because he will kill you for the mistake you made. Grace speaks the opposite. He will whisper to you through love that when you do mess up, you can run directly to your Father and he will help you. Whatever you have gotten yourself into, he is in the midst of it with you. You are not alone. As you walk, he walks because he's in you, so naturally he is going to support you moving into the right direction. The truth is within you, and the Father through the Son has lifted you up in him. Right now, you are on the same equal ground in the heavenly realm as Christ. You only need to remember who you are by looking to who Christ is and then think on him, living your life from out of him. There is no life in darkness. You have been given the full light within you, and there is no longer any need for you to remain outside in the cold when you are fully covered, warm, and on fire with the all-consuming love he has for you.

Your Father wants you all to himself in a one-on-one relationship that is personalized between you both. He has already prepared your life to live with him ahead of time. There is no need to struggle through wondering how to live right, just listen to his still quiet voice and let yourself be influenced into the rhythm of his moves. What an amazing gift God has given you, which is himself within. You never have to suffer under the anxieties of the world because we are saved from all hostility and totally encapsulated in his love.

I will finish this chapter with a message taken from Andre Rabe's book, *"Adventures in Christ."* This is a wonderful thought to meditate on that you are equal to God.

~ "Have the same attitude that Jesus had. He knew that he was equal to God, and this assurance gave him the confidence to be a servant without an inferiority complex. We don't have to justify or nervously defend this position of equality, for we have not promoted ourselves to this position. He made us this way! This awareness does not give us a superior attitude, but it is the very knowledge that sets us free to serve others with complete abandonment." Philippians 2:5-8 ~

Chapter 2

~Salvation~

"Are you tired? Worn out? Burned out on religion? Come to Me. Get away with Me and you'll recover your life. I'll show you how to take a real rest. Walk with Me and work with Me—watch how I do it. Learn the unforced rhythms of grace. I won't lay anything heavy or ill-fitting on you. Keep company with Me and you'll learn to live freely and lightly."
Jesus of Nazareth
Mo Thomas

The Good News of Salvation is the complete and finished work of Jesus Christ consisting of the inclusion of your life in his, apart from any of your own efforts. It's your revelation awareness that he completely accepts you, and it makes no difference if you believe in him or not. The fact is, it's all finished and done. The Father does not wait for our choice to save us; everything has already been fulfilled through his Son. The atonement was universal, and it was for every human even if you have never confessed your love for Jesus or if you believe.

Religious bondage has kept countless people separated from God in their mind through guilt, condemnation and fear by imprisoning us with its rituals that became so deeply ingrained that only his love has the all-consuming power to remove these oppressive strongholds. As we embark on our newfound freedom in love, all the rules and regulations we have been taught over time will often resurface and try to take hold of our minds again. The apostle Paul spoke about this very situation that he too faced when he encouraged the people at Philippi, and us today, to forget those things of the past as we reach forward.

"Brethren, I do not count myself to have apprehended, but one thing I do, forgetting those things which are behind and reaching forward to those things which are ahead." (Philippians 3:13)

Paul understood that the nature of religion is to put all the emphasis on what we must do right, instead of focusing our attention on what the Father has already done through the Son. The big hinge pin that religion swings from is to take control over people, which pushes all the buttons of fear to manipulate people. Through the eyes of religion and its twisted beliefs, this fear makes a person follow something above what Jesus has done and accomplished on our behalf, instead of ruling and reigning through being led by his Spirit. We have been taught that Jesus came to save us from hell, and if we don't come to him willingly and confess that we love and accept him with our mouth and then obey specific laws, we will be heading for hell. The blind guides have no awareness of his passionate wrath of love, and from this lack of knowing his unconditional love they stipulate conditions on us to choose Christ as Lord of our lives.

This is a human-made doctrine with worldly judgmental views on what they believe God has said to the entire human race. The apostle Paul is our New Testament theologian who was taught by the Holy Spirit directly, not through man-made doctrines; and he gives us a great example of how to walk by the Spirit of God in all of life's situations.

It is through our salvation that the teachers of religious law have their starting point to ensnare and rope us in through fear. It's a structure based on believing that we must do certain things and follow laws and rules to be saved and then to stay saved. We try to obey certain instructions in the hope of remaining secure in God, so we set out implementing plans to follow these specific guidelines. We don't want to displease God, and our hearts want to make him happy. And we certainly don't want to end up in this place of eternal conscious torment they call hell.

There is a constant underlying fear within religion that plagues our minds, causing us to constantly wonder if we are saved or if we are not saved. We believe there is a price to pay when we sin, so we cry, beg, condemn ourselves, and sulk in misery because of our wrong actions. Then one day we arise and start to feel good again, feeling confident that our suffering was enough to please God, and so we head off with him, happy until we do something wrong again. Then we repeat the whole cycle over again in a vicious circle. A constant internal warring is going on as we wonder whether we have done enough through our own efforts to please God, and if we obeyed adequately and followed the right rules so we can receive all the promises God has for us.

The whole thesis of religion is a matter of Salvation, and whether you have your ticket to heaven or a ticket to hell. In most religious circles, when we ask Jesus into our hearts and make him our personal Lord and Savior, we believe we have entered secure grounds that other people have not yet entered. The truth about every human's Salvation has nothing at all to do with doing or giving anything to Jesus. Salvation is all about what he has freely given to us, without stipulations or conditions. He has given to you everything now and eternally, free of charge without requiring anything in return. We read this in Romans chapter 8:32 where it says very simply, ***"He who did not spare his own Son, but delivered him up for us all, how shall he not with him also freely give us all things?"*** This Scripture clearly explains that we have been given Christ freely who is our Salvation. He does not require us to do anything because he has already done it all for us. In the original Greek, the word *all* as we read throughout Scripture means everybody without exception. Our Father delivered Christ up for *all* people at no charge, and by our being delivered up with Christ we also received all the benefits to everything that is in him. It is a final deal and there is no prayer you can say, nor anything you can possibly do to earn Salvation.

The objective of religion is to have our minds focused toward ourselves rather than emphasizing our attention and direction on the mind of Christ. He is the One who has completed everything for us and delivered us from our mind of darkness to his marvelous light. Paul explains this in Colossians 1:13 as we read, ***"He has delivered us from the power of darkness."*** That darkness Paul talks about is living in your mind absent from God. The darkened place in your mind is illuminated with the revelation light of Christ within you, and who you are as he is in this world. Once the light goes on, that darkness within you will disappear and you will come alive in the power of his mind. Paul explains that as our mind sees him it surpasses all knowledge, and his love has the all-consuming power that impresses on our hearts, resulting in our making the right decisions that will benefit ourselves and everyone around us.

"For who has known the mind of the Lord that he may instruct him? But we have the mind of Christ."
1 Corinthians 2:16

Paul continues in Colossians 1:13-14 and he says, ***"He has delivered us from the power of darkness and conveyed us into the kingdom of the Son of his love, in whom we have redemption through his blood, the forgiveness of sins."*** In other versions, in this passage the word for *conveyed* is the word *translated,* which in the original Greek is a powerful word that means *instantaneously.* Christ delivered us, which is the past tense, from the powers of being in the dark and alienated, alone without God. He transported us into the Kingdom of his dear Son and there's no stipulation on this action and no asterisk in the Bible where we look down to see if there is anything we need to add. There is nothing further you can do for your eternal life that is in him, which was totally visible and generated by God, that can be produced by your efforts or good deeds. As you surrender to him, his eternal life within you will be generated and made totally visible by his efforts, not yours. Surrendering to God is a complete rest from trying to please him in your own efforts. You are simply adjusting your focus and attention on him through a relationship where you are talking with him daily. He will respond, and as you hear his gentle loving promptings from within you, his love for you will compel you to naturally transform and take the desired right steps. There is a verse of Scripture in 1 Peter 1:3 that was a tremendous eye-opener and brought me out of a lot of error within my mind. ***"Blessed be the God and Father of our Lord Jesus Christ, who according to his abundant mercy has begotten us again to a living hope through the resurrection of Jesus Christ from the dead."*** The word *begotten* in the Greek is the word, *"Anagennao"* and it means; *produced again, to be born again, to be born anew.*

It is according to his abundant mercy that God has birthed every human again, enabling us to be born again to the living hope through the resurrection of Jesus Christ from the dead. People in the Old Testament were blind to their authentic identity as an image and likeness of God. They were looking through a glass clouded by tradition, culture, and even in some cases superstition learned from pagan religions.

Jesus came to clear the view, to uncloud the glass of how the Father should be seen, for both Jews and Gentiles. His resurrection birthed us ***all*** from death to life, opening our hearts to receive the Spirit of truth to lead us into all truth. There is one God and Father of ***all***, both pre and post cross. Jesus came to unveil to humanity who they had always been but were asleep to their reality.

When Christ resurrected, his Spirit went into all humans from the foundation of the world. Whether people were living or dead, or have yet to be born, all have his Spirit from the time of his ascension. In the Old Testament they only had a partial view because they had been looking to God on the outside. God's heart and love was not made clear on their hearts because Christ had not yet come. But the day Christ resurrected was the day that his Spirit entered ***all*** humanity from the past, present and future. (Romans 8:11) There were people who had the revelation of Christ within, but just as today, there were also some who did not experience him while they walked on the earth. However, we are assured that every knee will bow, and ***all*** humans will come to the realization of Christ within them, either on earth or in eternity. (Romans 14:11)

Every person on earth who has the revelation of Christ is a walking testimony of him, and Christ is going to keep drawing us closer to him and learning of him through our everyday life. I don't think we've given the resurrection the credibility it deserves as a life triggering event for all of humanity. We were all born again, according to 1 Peter 1:3, on the day that Jesus resurrected, and it had nothing to do with your confession of faith or your belief. ***"Blessed be the God and Father of our Lord Jesus Christ, who according to his abundant mercy has begotten us again to a lively hope through the resurrection of Jesus Christ from the dead."***

It is religion that is the criminal here by installing a set of beliefs deep into our consciousness that we must attain a set lifestyle of rules and rituals to make sure we are right with God. They promote that it is our doing that saves us and makes us secure in our salvation. This is the thief that comes to steal us away into a false teaching that when we do good and pleasing acts for God, and put on this fake performance of outer works, he must be pleased with us. We are under the false impression that I'm pleased with myself so therefore God must also be pleased with me! This is fake humility wrapped up in a false identify and beliefs that has its roots in a human made religious system.

In Philippians, Paul explains to us through his revelation that we must leave all the laws and the rules behind and never return to them. If we head back and return into bondage it will always hinder our path forward. Paul says in Philippians 3:12-15, ***"Not that I have already attained, or am already perfected; but I press on, that I may lay hold of that for which Christ Jesus has also laid hold of me. Brethren, I do not count myself to have apprehended; but one thing I do, forgetting those things which are behind and reaching forward to those things which are ahead, I press toward the goal for the prize of the upward call of God in Christ Jesus. Therefore, let us, as many as are mature, have this mind; and if in anything you think otherwise, God will reveal even this to you."***

It is really impossible to reach forward and know all the things that are ahead while we continue looking over our shoulder at what's behind us. There is an immeasurable amount of life-giving wonderful revelation that Christ wants to reveal to you as you step out each day in him. When we reflect back and choose to focus our mind on the past with all of its depression, we are actually projecting more of that same reality into our future. So long as we keep comparing ourselves and looking to religion as our measuring stick of performance for what is right and wrong, we bypass and detour away from the Spirit of Truth.

It is the Spirit that gives us life, and we don't find life from words written in a Bible that has been fabricated to mean something it was not intended to mean by religious teachers. Now don't get me wrong, the Bible is the best book in the world. It has tremendous revelation, however, as we read it, we receive revelation through our relationship with Christ as we mediate on what we are reading. The very words Jesus Christ speaks directly to you, is what gives you life, and they are not the words of someone else or written in the Bible. (John 5:39) He speaks to you from what you read, hear, and see throughout your daily life, and he who has ears to hear shall hear. (Matthew 11:15)

"It is the Spirit who gives life, the flesh profits nothing. The words that I speak to you are spirit, and they are life." John 6:63

If you still have one foot in religion, it's going to be difficult for you to move ahead. There is a preconceived concept that we already have all the revelation of truth from God that we need in the spiritual realm. We need to abandon that idea because God is never ending. The revelation is needed in your daily life just as much as you need a daily ration of water to survive. Truth and grace are the person of Jesus Christ, and he has a continuous stream of revelation for you that is eternal. We can far more easily receive the revelation of Christ by letting go of all the things that religion and the Christian mixed message has taught us and we once held onto, especially if it's rooted in fear. We attend church, believing it is the right thing to do and that this will make God happy. Through years of attendance and hearing a human made message, we come to believe we are the ones who need to initiate and petition for our own salvation. From these beliefs, we approach God with our prayers and confession, thinking it is *us* who accepts him into our hearts. We give ourselves all the credit and say, "I accepted Christ, I'm the hero here, and I did it!" Then we have this assumption that God unfolds his arms and reacts to us because of what we did. What an incredible failed system with completely false beliefs tied to it! The reality is, we have it wrong and backwards. I can best explain that we have all received salvation without the need to do anything through Scripture. In 1 John 4:19 he says, ***"We love him because he first loved us."***

All we did was respond to his love, and he initiated this with all the love that he has for us first. It was not our decision to do something that made him love us. The idea has been drilled into us that we must kneel down at the altar and tell him how much we love him and thank him for dying on the cross for us, and then he accepts our own individual invitation. This is the backward teaching that we have come to understand.

It is us coming to him through a loving relationship from his invitation to us that we respond from out of his love, grace, and mercy. In John 15:16 Christ said, ***"You didn't choose Me, but I chose you."*** That is an earth-shaking revelation for most of us to hear because we thought we chose him. Christ said, ***"You did not choose Me but I chose you and appointed you that you should go and bear fruit, and that your fruit should remain that whatever you ask the Father in My name He may give you."***

Our fruit is borne out of the revelation that we receive from him as we communicate with him daily. Wc approach God with an open childlike heart that is curious to know truth, and hungry to know him intimately. We come to him in all eagerness, with a receptive attitude that allows an answer to be received. If we come with anxiety and fear, this can often block our pathways to hearing, believing, and then receiving. When you come to God asking and then hear him, that revelation goes into your heart; and it is from your heart that you believe and then receive. It is a natural response of believing; it's like turning a light on and removing yourself from darkness. As you hear the truth and it penetrates your heart, the next natural thing to do is to respond through words and actions.

At times in my life there have been tough situations where I just couldn't seem to find an answer to the problem. It was during those times that I ran to my Father and talked to him about it. Then I was able to leave, secure in the knowledge that I will receive my answer. In God's time I will receive the revelation on the truth of that situation, which will come into my spirit from God's Spirit within me. God has the answer and He is not taking his time to reveal it to me however, I may have to wait till I am open to receiving what he wants me to know. Perhaps I might still be too focused on the problem to see the answer that is already there. Either way, he answered. God does not withhold his promises; he will provide a way through any situation that we are facing, he has all the answers, and it has all been done for us, even before we ask.

"Therefore, do not be like them, for your Father knows the things you have need of before you ask him."
Matthew 6:8

Jesus called all of his twelve disciples, it was not them who choose him, just as he has called every person that ever existed. He came and offered us the invitation, and we reacted and responded, which is believing, and responding to his invitation. You cannot generate belief from out of yourself. It is a simple effortless response to the revelation of Christ. Think of times when people tried to get you to believe something, yet you weren't going to allow yourself to be forced into agreeing with something you didn't believe! This is exactly what happened in the life of Paul. In Acts 9:6 it says, ***"So he, trembling and astonished, said, Lord, what do You want me to do? Then the Lord said to him, Arise and go into the city, and you will be told what you must do."*** Paul believed through his response to Christ, who spoke to him through his spirit. It was a Spirit to spirit conversation that hit Paul's heart dead on, and from there it moved up to his mind where he then responded.

Paul was trembling and astonished. This was not the result of anything generated by Paul, who then said, "Lord what do you want me to do?" I maintain today that every one of us who have come to a genuine encounter with the living Lord Jesus Christ, it was not because we went to him and told him how much we loved him, and how much we wanted to be saved. It was because he made himself known to us, and we responded to him by believing. It's not something we can do ourselves, and neither can we generate the faith for our salvation. Faith means; *to have confidence in the One who promised it and having the ability to also make it happen.* This means that it is not your faith, it is Christ's faith. He is the One who makes it all happen and there is nothing any of us can do.

I remember back in my word of faith days, I would try to build up my faith because we heard them preach that faith comes by hearing and hearing by the word; and that's true. However, the word you hear should generate a trust in the One who gave you the word, and I'm not talking about the preacher. It is Christ who gives the word, but despite this, I would try to develop my own faith, which is really me trying to develop confidence in myself. I tried to generate my own faith by confessing the Scripture in the Bible, and I had a whole lot of sheets of Scripture I used to pin up around the house and confess over and over. In my early years, I was a big Charles Capps follower and I read his book on *Creative Power* and what he called *"Goss Pills!"* I would take those *"Goss Pills"* every day by confessing certain Scriptures, because faith would come by hearing the word of God. I was trying to generate my own faith and build my faith up, so that I could receive what I thought I needed. Little did I know, that's not how faith comes!

I eventually came to the revelation knowledge that's not what Biblical faith means. Faith is a trust in the One who made the promise, and that he has the ability, the power, and the strength to fulfill all his promises. We don't need to look too far for our leading example in the Bible. Consider Abraham, who is the father of our faith. Abraham demonstrated how we are to rely, communicate, and live out our relationship through love with our Father. I know that many people reading this have come through a variety of spiritual gymnastics to build up faith, and in so doing, you have now become weak, tired and exhausted, which is exactly why Jesus said in Matthew 11:28 (paraphrased), ***"Come to Me, all of you who are weary and burdened, and I will give you rest,"*** and don't we need his rest after so many years in religious bondage!

We have tried desperately to become spiritual giants and great people of faith just like we see with televangelists. Yet they are not our guides against whom we are to measure how our own faith is going. It is Christ as he reveals the living word to us. In Romans 4:17, God spoke to Abraham, and at this time he did not have a Bible to go to and search out the Scriptures. He was hearing God through his own spirit talking to him. God said he would make Abraham a father of many nations, yet how could Abraham do this when he was an old man and didn't have any children. So, what did Abraham have to do to receive this promise? He did the only thing any of us need to do, and that is to trust in the ability and power of the One who made the promise. We can see through reading this Scripture in Romans 4:17 that it had nothing to do with what Abraham could do. He didn't need to build his faith and confess the Scriptures over and over because there was no written Scripture to confess! He was the father of faith because he heard God through his spirit, and from out of his relationship with God, he trusted him. The Scripture says in Romans 4:17, ***"I have made you a father of many nations in the presence of him whom he believed – God, who gives life to the dead and calls those things which do not exist as though they did."***

Abraham believed what God told him was true; he didn't believe in his own ability to pull it off. That's what we thought faith was, we believed that faith was having to trust in our ability to produce the promises. After I learned God made me a promise, I used to search out something related to that promise in the Scriptures. Then, as we used to say in the word of faith days, I would *"Stand on that Scripture promise."* I reminded God of what he promised me, and I showed him where it was in the Scriptures and since God can't lie, it was my obligation to make this promise come to pass! I was trying to obtain promises in my own efforts through prayer and confession of the Scriptures by reading them over and over. Whatever it was, it was my responsibility to make sure my faith was big enough, and strong enough until the promise came to pass.

This is a major error that has circulated through the churches for far too many years now, that we must believe just as though I am God, and I will bring it to pass through my prayer and confession. This is believing in yourself. This is not believing in Christ as the One who has done it all. It is a false mindset that says, if it's going to happen then it will come to pass when my faith is right. If only I could get my faith right, I will have... And that list of *have's* goes on and doesn't stop. You will find yourself burning out in your own effort to try and build your faith and get what it is you think you need. This is not the correct way to understand faith. What a heavy burden it is doing all that in your own strength! There is no rest in Christ when you have to run off and try to obtain promises that you already have in him. As we live in communication with Christ and hear him through our spirit, he meets all our needs, and we receive them effortlessly as we rest in our heavenly revelation.

In Romans 4:18 we read, ***"Who, contrary to hope, in hope believed, so that he became the father of many nations, according to what was spoken, so shall your descendants be."*** It all came to pass according to what God said to Abraham. It was by God's ability, not anything that Abraham did on his own. He continues to say in Romans 4:19-22, ***"And not being weak in faith, he did not consider his own body, already dead since he was about 100 years old, and the deadness of Sarah's womb. He did not waver at the promise of God through unbelief, but was strengthened in faith, giving glory to God, and being fully convinced that what He had promised He was also able to perform. And therefore, it was accounted to him for righteousness."***

Religion keeps us in a spirit of constant work, making believing in faith something you have to muster up and continue to work at in order for you to keep receiving. The fact is, when we awaken to truth that has always been, genuine belief and trust in God will then naturally start to spring up like a never-ending water fountain in a dry desert. We won't thirst any longer, we will just rest and listen to God and then respond to what we hear. Religion blocks the voice of God. When we operate from out of works and look to what the rules say, we have stepped away from hearing what God has for our lives. The Bible is a great source of wisdom. However, the words alone cannot produce any rest or change. In fact, if you are not walking in God's Spirit then reading some of the words in the Bible can create anxiety in you. You want to try and do your best to come to some level of perfection that you believe you must meet in order to be right with God. It is by hearing from his Spirit that resides in you and is connected to your spirit that the word is illuminated and comes alive like a two-edged sword, and once that word has been revealed and penetrates the heart, effortless change occurs. Stay in Spirit and resting in the Lord to reveal to you his Truth is trusting and believing in him, for what he says to you will be done. Religion brings unease. There is no rest because you are constantly trying to attain some measure of what is right in your mind. Living from his Spirit you come alive, and in that a calm resting will be produced.

When we rest in Christ, we cease from our own hard labors of struggling and striving that cause anxiety. Rest means we are calm within, and we wait on Christ within until we receive instruction and knowing the direction we must take. When the Lord begins to direct you, then you move. When the Lord speaks to you, then you speak. When he gives you an action to take, you then take that action. It won't be because it's a law or a ritual that you have an obligation to do, the action will be from knowing and wanting to respond from what you heard that empowered you. Whenever I've been anxious, I can devise ten plans to solve the dilemma, hoping to coil my anxiety. The more I follow my own divisive plans that, of course, won't work because God didn't speak them into me, the more anxious I become. I eventually have to come back to the place of rest, which is in him, and talk to God and settle myself down.

"Religion wants to Break you... the Spirit of Truth wants to Awaken you..."

One of the main assurance's God has given us is that we're not walking through this thing alone. We're never by ourselves, I don't care how it looks, you are not alone. Jesus was not by himself when he hung on the cross. The

Father was in Christ, reconciling the world to himself, so, everything Jesus went through the Father went through.

Everything you're going through he's going through it with you, as he has with you in the past. Resting is where you cease from your labors, trusting is where you just lean back into his arms and tell yourself, "Look, the Father's got this." Belief is not so much an action as it a response, believing is a response to revelation or a response to what he's showing you. When he shows me something I'm not worn out, I'm not tired, I'm not emotionally drained because I've been resting. So, when he shows me what I need to do, I'm able to respond to it for I have the strength and energy to carry on with it.

Paul talks about how to deal with life's anxieties in Philippians in 4:6-7. ***"Be anxious for nothing, but in everything by prayer and supplication, with thanksgiving, let your requests be made known to God, and the peace of God, which surpasses all understanding, will guard your hearts and minds through Christ Jesus."*** You will no longer have anxiety when you come to God and just talk with him, which is prayer and thanksgiving, and letting him know what your requests are, those things which are on your mind. Once you have talked to God about the situation, a peace will come to you within your spirit. God will be answering you, and this will surpass all of what you understood about that situation. He is going to reveal the answer in a way that will guard your heart and allow you to know the correct way to handle the situation. When he speaks to you it automatically eliminates anxiety, but when you speak to yourself and get caught up in all the fear of the situation, it will produce stress in your life.

Religion cannot produce the peace in your life that Christ can by following his Spirit, peace will cut anxiety off. When you allow peace to begin flooding your life, you will get ahold of yourself and begin to rest. You begin to trust and to simply believe.

You take a deep breath and let that peace come back in, and the peace Paul refers to in Philippians 4:7 is the peace of God which passes all understanding. Your mind, that had been all upset and going crazy, will now give you peace when you rest in him. Christ will guard your heart and your mind. Religion will push you to try through your effort, which will result in a lot of anxiety. Jesus himself is going to come and minister his peace to you. In Ephesians 2:8-9, Paul encourages us through this Scripture that it is through our confidence in Christ that we will have the peace and security that we don't have while our minds are under the control of religion. ***"For by grace you have been saved through faith, and not of yourselves; it is the gift of God, not of works, lest anyone should boast."***

It is the wonderful gift of God that saves you. It is he who brings you into his arms and fills you with his love, and there are no words in any book, including the Bible, that can do that. There is only One who has the empowering love that transforms all our understanding, and it is through his Spirit that we are alive. You believed out of a response to his love for you that has always been. There has never been a time that he has not loved you. God has enabled you to believe, and it was not by your efforts. The church has taught us that we must strengthen our faith, and if you're not healed then it's your fault, because if only you had enough faith you could receive healing, or anything else you want.

Paul explains that it is not anything that any human can do. There is no contribution that you made at all. You have all the faith that you are ever going to receive, and it is Christ in you, the hope of glory. There is no human who can stand up in front of people and force anyone to believe, no matter how much fear they promote with the false doctrine of hell. They command people to say a line of words so they will not enter eternal conscious torment in a place called hell. If you ever enter a church and they feed you the line that if you don't do as they stipulate then you are going to hell, I will give you the same good advice Paul did to the Galatian church: Run away as quick as you can! Run, and never go back! The fact is hell does not exist and you can read all the truth about hell in my book; *"Hell's Illusion."* Anybody who has confessed to the preacher or themselves a few lines of words didn't believe in anything. They had no revelation of the Father, and they only confessed out of fear, and we know that there is no love in fear. It is not a place where God resides. Religion is going to keep promoting this because it produces too much money for them to stop. When you have people in fear, they are going to come to you and be under your influence while they await your commands on how to eliminate their fear and prevent an unfavorable outcome. How we feel on the inside will have a major impact on how we see our Father.

Your believing is an effortless response to his overwhelming love for you, and the very image of Christ is the image of who you are, as Francois Du Toit beautifully paraphrases in the *"Mirror Bible"* in Ephesians 4:21 and 5:14. I will leave this chapter with something for you to ponder.

~ "It is not possible to study Christ in any other context, he is the incarnation, hear him resonate within you! The truth about you has its ultimate reference in Jesus, he did not come to introduce a new compromised set of rules, he is not an example for us but of us!"

"This is the message of light; Christ awakens you from your intoxicated slumber and resurrects you out of the death trap of enslaved thought patterns." ~

Chapter 3

~Adamic Nature~

"The God Adam created in his mind was served for generations until Abba said enough!...and came himself in a earth suit, to show for all to see his love and inclusion of All in his family...It seems many are still serving the angry, punitive, judgmental God of Adam's mental construct."
Don Keathley

We have been taught to not take any responsibility for ourselves because it's not our fault. After all, we were born with an Adamic nature and we can't be blamed for that since it's just the way we are. Once we learn the truth in knowing that we do not have an Adamic nature and can completely go to our Father at any time through anything we do, good or bad, it completely transforms our lives. We are then responding to God out of a relationship, not through hiding and being distant.

I was very fortunate while growing up. I had a great father and stepfather who took care of me. I knew that even if I fouled up, I could call them, and they would listen with understanding. I wasn't fearful, for I recognized they would be there for me. This is just like our Father. I had the security in knowing that I could call my father at any time because we had such a great relationship, enabling me to know his heart for me with confidence and no doubt, which is the same response we have with our Father. Having an individual relationship with him will create within us no hesitation and uncertainty. Every person will have a tempting thought at some time in their life, or throughout the day. The issue of separation can feel evident within us when we act on that tempting desire. In James 1:14, he describes it as being drawn away. Once we act upon this, we can sense within ourselves when we have made a wrong move, that our actions are not in line with something good and beneficial that the Father has for us, so we condemn ourselves and then believe that it is of God. There are consequences for all actions, be it good or bad, and the results are wrong actions and the wages of sin, which is death, that comes from the sin itself. It doesn't come from the Father's punishment. In Romans 5:12, Paul says, much the same thing, as we read, ***"Therefore, just as through one man sin entered the world, and death through sin, and thus death spread to all men, because all sinned."*** Paul explains that death spread to all men, it was not Adam who caused and made people to sin. People chose for themselves to copy his faulty actions and mindset separation to go their own way separate from God. Adam planted this propensity in nature that showed separation was possible if a person removes themselves away from God through the mind, but there is no evidence to suggest that he caused all people to be separated. Paul's remarkable encounter with Christ within had him totally convinced that there is no separation from the love of God, and that we are always connected to him.

"For I am persuaded, that neither death, nor life, nor angels nor principalities nor powers, nor things present nor things to come, nor height nor depth, nor any other created thing, shall be able to separate us from the love of God which is in Christ Jesus our Lord."
Romans 8:38

The truth is, in God's perspective nothing can separate you from him, ever. And there is no Adamic nature. Sin does not remove people from the love that God has for you. God looks at us with no separation, even if we mess up and do the wrong things, which we all do at times; yet we can always come boldly to our Father and talk with him. It is us humans that have the feeling, brought on by wrong thinking, that leads us to believe we need to hide. There is no such thing as a sin nature that has been deposited onto all of humanity because of Adam. Jesus and the apostles never taught this doctrine, which has been conjured up and mistranslated by religious people who want to add on their own agendas to program people's lives.

The Adamic made-up story was created from mankind's selfish desires to use fear to exercise control. People then use this teaching as a type of victim mentality where they think this is their way to escape being responsible for their actions and having to come before God. All that we ever need to do is come to our Father, be humble and admit that we have made a few mistakes and some wrong turns. If you come to him openly and admit that you made a wrong turn in life, he is going to help you turn everything around for the better and correct all wrongs as you continue to learn through his teaching.

God cannot be separate from love for that is impossible. Only humans know how to do this, which was demonstrated by Adam, until Jesus Christ came and showed us the right actions and how to live following God.

In Colossians 1:21-22, we read, ***"And you, who once were alienated and enemies in your mind by wicked works, yet now he has reconciled in the body of his flesh through death, to present you holy, and blameless, and above reproach in his sight."***

Our wicked works can make us feel as though we are alienated, and sometimes what we do is not that wicked. Even so, we know when we have departed from hearing God and stepped out on our own. Once we step out, isolated in our minds, we can get right into our own wants and desires that may come at the price of our walk with God and with other people. Our remedy is Christ, who has reconciled us to him blameless and above reproach in his sight. (Colossians 1:22) We need to take note of what Paul is saying in his revelation, that it is *in his sight that we are blameless.* So no matter what people tell you about yourself, and perhaps they have an old picture of who you used to be, it makes no difference what people think of you. In God's eyes, just as Christ is, you are in this world. You can hold your head up high because in him is where you have all the victory, and as Paul says in 1 Corinthians 5:17, you are now a new creation, the old has gone. You can tell people that you don't know who that old person is anymore because you are too busy rejoicing in the new person in Christ!

Sometimes when we eat of the tree of the knowledge of good and evil it can really affect our minds and egos, which then results in our feeling like we are separated. It is a fact that Adam was the one who introduced a bend in our thinking that led to wrong actions that gave us the sense of a disconnection in our walk with God. The separation was actually a lie and an illusion, and it was the same lie that Adam suffered from.

"It is our perception that creates our reality."

If we are raised in a family who believes we are totally depraved and born with a sin nature, an Adamic nature, they will pass that lie onto us until the day we have the revelation of truth. We have been told lies that we are born sinners and are heading for some place called hell for all eternity. But just because that was our perception doesn't mean it's true.

Jesus, the apostles, and the disciples never taught the Adamic separation to people. If you go before the foundation of the world you will see that you were placed in Christ before you were ever lost in Adam. In Ephesians 1:4 we read, ***"Just as he chose us in him before the foundation of the world, that we should be holy and without blame before him in love."*** This gives us a tremendous amount of security, knowing that we have always been in Christ. This is where we are sealed and secured, and nobody can tell you otherwise. This is your position that you are never coming out of.

Those who believe in a sin nature always come back to one common verse that religious people like to speak about to tell us that all humans are born in sin. This verse is found in Psalm 51:5 where David said, ***"Behold I was brought forth in iniquity and in sin, my mother conceived me."*** This is the point they say, *"See right there it says in sin my mother conceived me."* Do you think this Scripture is talking about David being a sinner at the point of conception? Or is it in sin my mother conceived me? Or could it be the condition of the mother when she conceived David? If you do a little bit of historical study, you will find that David's father was not Abigail's first husband. According to some historians, Abigail had a checkered past, however, this is not entirely clear. I am going to replace the word sin in Psalm 51:5, to read *"In blindness my mother conceived me."* Would you think that David was blind from the point of conception? Or would you think it was relating to the condition of the mother? If the verse said, *"In poverty my mother conceived me,"* would you think that David was poor from his mother's womb? Or maybe he was speaking about his mother being poverty stricken? We can add any word in there that we like such as anger, fear, insecurity, happiness, or in joy my mother conceived me. I think the preponderance of evidence is that David knew something about his mom, and we cannot say without any shadow of a doubt that this verse was speaking about David being in sin from the point of conception. The Scripture is pointing more toward the condition of the mother, which I think becomes very clear when you place another word in there for sin.

Religious teaching will always start with the problem and the sin nature. They teach us that we are separated from God and he is angry with us. It is a self-perpetuated illusion. God had the solution before there was a problem. If you look at Adam and sin as the problem, then I don't think we are looking far enough back to what God provided as a solution.

If we go back to Genesis 2:7 we are going to read how it all started and see if we came into this world with a sin nature. ***"And the Lord God formed man of the dust of the***

ground, and breathed into his nostrils the breath of life; and man became a living being."

Did man come into existence with a sin nature? Absolutely not. Humans came into existence with a divine nature. God breathed into all people the breath of life. It was God's very breath, his deity of being divine, God breathed into human's eternal life. That is the breath of God. There is nothing that ever took away that breath, and there is nothing that would lead us to believe what God breathed into humans at the beginning was ever taken away.

The question may still be on your mind; *are we separated from God?* Jesus said in John 14:20, ***"At that day you will know that I am in My Father, and you are in Me, and I in you."*** Jesus was bringing the absolute point of our security for us to know that there is no separation. There is an absolute union that he is in the Father; and we are in him, and he is in us, and we are joined together with all humanity as one in the Father and the Son. That day was the very day that Christ ascended, and his Spirit went out and into all of humanity, and that day came for you in the form of remembrance when you had the revelation of Christ in you. That was the day you knew without any doubt that the Christ Spirit is within you, and he is in the Father and you are in him.

The mind of sin consciousness separation that we have been taught has to go because it has held us back from believing we have access to the Father at any time. Jesus didn't come to embed sin consciousness. Jesus came to entrench within us Son consciousness, and there is a tremendous world of difference between the two.

Religion likes to impart and incriminate people with their angry God theory, so this begs the question, is God really angry and upset with us? Jeremiah the prophet said, ***"For I know the thoughts that I think towards you, says the Lord, thoughts of peace and not of evil, to give you a future and a hope." (Jeremiah 29:11)***

In just that one verse I don't see an angry God from the beginning. I see a God that says, *"I know my mind towards you, and I know what I think about you, and they are thoughts of peace, and it is not of any evil."* The whole lie of religion is an identity issue, which is who you are in Christ. Religion has always wanted to secure your identity at the fall of Adam. When you look back through your life in church, the starting point is always Adam and the fall. It is interesting because there was not one person who could ever give you the verse that actually says, *"You have a sin nature!"* There was never any verse given to you that said, *"You have an Adamic nature."* Where was the verse that tells us we were born separated from God? It is nowhere to be found, and none of the teachers and pastors in churches today can ever provide you with an exact Scripture that says any of this. They conveniently twist the Scriptures to suit them. They influence our minds and we then trust and believe what they say.

Have you ever taken your newborn baby home then looked at him or her in the eyes and said, *"You little depraved demon baby, if you don't get your life right you will be heading straight to hell!"* Why would we think that? The little baby is innocent, there is not an inkling of anything evil in that child. If you believe that you are depraved and born into this world with a sin nature, and that God is going to be angry at you if you don't do certain things, you will always be off center. You would be living your life as a lie in the wrong identity of who you really are in God. Sadly, many people are still living under this lie, which is why it is so important for you and me to help people be set free. Too many people today are still eating from the tree of knowledge of good and evil, and judging themselves through the lens of an Adamic nature. We read in Jeremiah 29:11, our identity by which we need to see ourselves. Identity is learning and having the revelation of how God sees you through his eyes of divinity, which is perfect and wonderful; and just as Jesus is in this world, so are you.

We quoted and talked about Ephesians 1:4-5 (paraphrased), which reads, ***"Just as he chose us in Him before the foundation of the world, he predestined us to adoption as sons."*** That is your predestination, all humans have been adopted as sons and daughters of God. We have the Christ Spirit within us, and he is your identity. We are adopted to Jesus Christ himself, according to the good pleasure of his Will and it was not your will, nor anything you did or could ever do. Then we read Paul saying in Ephesians 1:11, ***"In him also we have obtained an inheritance, being predestined according to the purpose of him who works all things according to the counsel of his will."*** This is what you don't hear in church, that this is your identity. Instead, what they push is that God is angry with you, and you are separated from him because we are all born with an Adamic nature. In Christ you have everything, it is only once we decide to step out in our own desires and wants that we fall victim to the world. Once we start living by the world's standards, we are subject to what the world offers, which is predominately riddled with anxieties and problems. However, remaining in Christ always ensures that you have the victory. You have peace and joy when you are in the Lord, even while in the midst of a bad situation, the joy is not the situation. Of course, it is painful and may be very uncomfortable. But the joy you have is knowing that you are seated with Christ in the heavenly realm, which is him, and that you are an overcomer because he is in you, and he has overcome the world. So, as you remain in him, you will not be like the world and suffer in anxiety because he provides the way out for you.

Your mind is going to turn towards the way of the world at times, but when you do something that you realize after the fact you shouldn't have done, your mind will then try to separate you from God. We have all experienced this, and it's through learning and coming to the revelation that God is love, that you will know your loving Father wants nothing but the best for you. When you know his unconditional love for you, then automatically no matter what happens, you know that you can always run to him. We don't need to run from God since he knows everything anyway, and he wants to help us. Even if you have a wrong desire, don't run off in the wrong direction, thinking that he won't notice and you can do whatever you want. Remember, he wants you to have the best life, he wants you to have everything that is good and beneficial. If there is a strong desire in you, then go to your Father and talk to him openly about it. He is there for you and he will listen and direct you regarding that situation, and he will help you see that it is not profitable for you. Once you receive the truth on the matter, that desire and temptation will leave you. It was probably going to ruin you in some way, so why take a destructive road when you can have the best road ever and have success. Religion teaches you to hide from God and pretend that you are not tempted and don't have any bad desires. Maybe you don't, but I think it is safe to say that inside every human there are selfish desires, and if we act on them it can lead us into all kinds of situations that will not be good. Grace allows you and God to be one together, and to share this life and talk about everything together, and then allow God to direct your path.

Our minds might pull us towards the tree of knowledge and good and evil. We can be very self-determining at times because most of us have been raised with this belief in human-made religion. Once we realize that we are heading away from grace, we can straightaway return without any guilt or condemnation. Even though Adam and many of us have eaten from the wrong tree, that has not dissuaded God nor convicted him to produce in us a plan *B!* Jesus was not God's plan *B*. Jesus was always plan *A* and he was always coming in the likeness of man, to show us himself how unified he was with us, and that he always wanted to be one with all humanity.

I think when Adam was hiding from God in the bushes, he was wondering how he could bring himself back into a right position because he knew his mind had taken a detour into some sort of mess. The truth is, he never lost the position which is why God went looking for him. God was not angry with him. He didn't approach Adam with fury or hostility. Instead, God approached Adam with love and acceptance. He protected Adam and moved him out of the garden so he would not be fooled by that illusion forever. God's love for you is dynamic, and I really want you to receive the open invitation of his intoxicating love.

I will complete this chapter with a reading from, *"Beyond an Angry God,"* by Steve McVey, a tremendous book which outlines God's great passionate love for you.

~ "God didn't pour out anger against Jesus on the cross, just as the Old Testament high priest didn't pour out anger against a lamb on the mercy seat. Propitiation was remedial, not retributive! The cross was the place of divine agape, not divine anger! The only anger at Calvary was the anger of sinful humanity unleashed on Pure Love. The cross of Jesus Christ is the purest expression of love that has ever existed or will ever exist. In that place of propitiation, as Pure Agape submitted himself to the ferocity of sinful humanity, he also absorbed our sin into his own body and soul so that we would be delivered from its consequences. Your God wasn't angry with Jesus, and he isn't anger with you." ~

Chapter 4

~Age of Accountability~

"Religion believes that you made God your Father by your faith. The Gospel is believing God made you his child by his faith."
Matthew Knickle

Religion teaches us that we must accept Jesus into our hearts at the very point in which we understand our need to do so, and this could possibly be as young as eight years old. The false religious doctrine I am exposing in this chapter is the so-called *"Age of accountability"* founded under the illusion that we are separated from birth from our eternal Spirit Father. This damnable doctrine tells us that we are born with a sinner's nature and separated from God, and that we have an Adamic nature, and we're headed for hell.

It is an atrocity even to think, teach, or consider for one minute that if a child does not believe in Jesus and has never said the prayer, and something happens to them, they will be heading for hell. It is child abuse, to say the least, for any parent to ever harm their own child and burn them in a never-ending torture chamber. To even explain such evil things to a child is cruel, for it provokes all kinds of fears into their young minds that they will go on to carry throughout life. There is no fear in perfect love whatsoever, and we have no right to be teaching our children the horrors of what their natural eternal Father will do to them if they do not comply and mouth a few words. We see the same teachings demonstrated throughout most churches worldwide for children and adults who do not believe in Jesus Christ. The Apostle Paul never taught this heresy. Honestly, if you believe such a horrific doctrine, then you would have to say that abortion is the best solution so that no child or adult could potentially burn in hell for all eternity. I would rather never have children than to have them, only for them to be tortured in a place called hell for all eternity. God has given us the gift of children so we can love and enjoy them. He did not make the ability to produce humans in his image so he can bless some and torture others. God's intention was always to have a relationship with his children, and for all of humanity to walk in love throughout life and have enjoyment with him. That is the very reason and purpose we are all created, to be in a relationship with God and have joy while walking out our lives through his love.

Many people are stuck in the wrong place and live a life driven by fear based on all manner of addictions because they are alone. They do not know love, and if they don't know the true love that the Father has for them, they will misuse the life God gave them to enjoy. A life absent from love is a life driven by a false sense of reality produced out of fear.

"Religion strives, confesses, believes, tries to muster up enough faith, to deserve a relationship with the Father. Grace brings to remembrance a relationship you have always had with him since before the foundation of time."

The doctrine of an age of accountability was created by religion through self-seeking humans wanting to spread fear and lies, so they can control the masses and collect a money ransom to get you out of hell. Let's look at the damaging results from teaching these horrendous lies and just how harmful and deadly the mind can be when it is absent from his love. This example will show you just how sick and twisted a wrong belief can be in all its delusions brought on through incorrect teachings and mental separation from the love of God. It is so important that you not only have the revelation of the truth of grace and unconditional love, but that you share it with many people around you and help set the captives free.

A lady named Andrea Yates, from Texas drowned her five children who were all under the age of ten, on June 20th, 2001, in a bathtub for the very reason of age accountability. She wanted to ensure that her children would go to heaven instead of possibly dying and going to hell if they grow up not believing in Jesus Christ. Andrea really believed she was saving them from a worse death of eternal hellfire punishment for all eternity if she killed them before they reached the age of accountability. This is one of many stories happening all around the world today with people having delusional thinking, separate from the love of God. It is not only going on with people who are being taught these damaging religious doctrines, we can see the absence of God's love throughout the world in all kinds of horrendous evil attacks. The majority of evil thinking and acts are a response to the absence of the reality of God's unconditional love. The perpetrators were sane normal people who held strong self-deceptive fear-based beliefs, and in other cases there may be medical mind conditions. For those who find themselves in either extreme, love is the healing power for the mind and then it's received throughout the body. No parent can assume that just because they follow the Lord Jesus Christ that their children will do the same, no matter how much they have been taught about Jesus Christ. When they are an adult, they will decide what they will do with their lives, and it is terrible to think that your child could grow up and enter into hell because they chose not to follow Christ. So, by believing in this dangerous doctrine, wouldn't you assume Andrea did the right thing by protecting her kids from hell?

Of course, she did not do the right thing and there is no place in your heart of love that could ever think or do such a thing. We are made in the image of unconditional love, and in love, there is no torment and no harm. We instinctively and logically know this, and people who harm others do not know the depth of the Father's love for them. In Romans 8:31-39, Paul said the love of God could never leave us, and it can never be separated from us. Yet, if you believe in the separation of man and God from birth taught by religion, you will spend eternity separated without any option. The age of accountability doctrine teaches us that death is the end of the story, and although you may live a long life of over 100, the choices you make are irreversible and have separated you from the love of God that never fails. God is love, and he only has love for you, which has never left you. It was installed in you before the foundation of the world; and before you ever entered the world, you have been in eternity within your Father's love.

"What, then shall we say to these things? If God is for us, who can be against us?"
Romans 8:31

Do you see how ironic this is? His love never fails, it wins regardless of any timeframe because we are eternal beings. However, according to this doctrine, love fails, and you will be stuck in hell because of what you have not done, which is accept Jesus into your heart, and for all eternity you are now going to suffer for your wrong choice. That sounds like pure madness, and it's really hard to believe. So you can see how good these influential people are at fooling us and making us scared and fearful about God.

God cannot be love and also torture and separate you for a gazillion years for a wrong choice or a lack of choice that you made on a blip screen of eternity. The true teacher who resides in you, the Holy Spirit, will confirm what you are hearing. In Revelation 21:25, we read, ***"Its gates shall not be shut at all by day, there shall be no night there."*** It is all self-explanatory right here that God's gates will never be shut, and that death of the body is not the end of the story. We read in Revelation 21:8, ***"But the cowardly, unbelieving, abominable, murderers, sexually immoral, sorcerers, idolaters, and all liars shall have their part in the lake which burns with fire and brimstone, which is the second death."*** In these two verses, (and in Revelation 22:15-17) we read the people on the outside of the gates, those who practice sorcery, the sexually immoral, the murderers, the idolaters, and anyone who is a lover of doing wrong, when these people eat of the tree of life and do the commandments, they will enter into the city's gates. The gates are open, and they never shut, but some people have chosen to be on the outside of the gates, and these are the same people who earlier in the book of Revelation were thrown into the lake of fire.

The lake of fire was a fire of purification, not a fire of eternal damnation. However, mysteriously if you believe that it is a fire of eternal damnation, how did these people jump out of the lake of fire, and outside of the city's gates? So, to paint a picture, we have the liars, the sorcerers, the murderers, and those who never prayed the prayer, and who never believed and accepted Jesus; they are now outside the city. The gates are open, and the Spirit and the bride are saying to the people to come on in, and let all people who thirst and whoever desires, let them take the water of life freely. In Romans 8:38-39, we also read that there is no end to our existence in our Father even once the body has died. ***"For I am persuaded that neither death nor life, nor angels nor principalities nor powers, nor things present nor things to come, nor height nor depth, nor any other created thing, shall be able to separate us from the love of God which is in Christ Jesus our Lord."***

Paul is convinced and fully persuaded, which means he has no doubt that we will never be separated from God's love, even after death. Paul has explained everything that we go through in life: there is no angel or demon, and the Greek word for demon is the word *daimonion.* That word *daimonion* in the era that Christ used this word, in the Greek means *a conscious thought*. Christ used *daimonion* in the same way he used *pneuma,* which means in the Greek, wind, or breath, the breath of life. It is a word that best describes a non-material form of life. So here we read that not even your wrong thoughts can keep you from the presence of God's love for all eternity.

There is no power other than the power of Christ and God's Spirit, which resides in every human, so, therefore, there is no power of any kind that can ever keep you away from God's love. There would be no power that could ever take you away from the love you have for your children. No matter what they do in life or how many bad things they have done, they will always be your children that you wanted because of your love for them. Our Father is exactly the same. No matter how much religious bondage takes ahold of you, or how many bad things you think you have thought or done, he is forever going to be calling you into the arms of his never-ending, all-consuming, empowering, passionate love. His love is relentless, and it is a love that always wins. It may not be in our human timeframe, but God has said that every knee will bow and that love never fails.

Do I personally believe you need to make a decision for Jesus? Yes, absolutely. I don't believe anybody can reside in the heavenly realm without Jesus Christ. He is the only way, the truth, and the life, and every human has his Spirit within them. He is the One who lights our path, so how can we know the correct way to go if we don't come to the One who created us and knows the exact right path to walk on? We can't. We would be stumbling around in the dark as we try to make a way through our own strength. Christ is seated in the heavenly realm. We have every opportunity to enter willingly, and we do so by believing in Jesus Christ and walking out our life through a relationship with him. I believe the gates never shut, and every human can enter and share with Christ, in his life that is full of joy, any time they willingly decide to change their mind and turn to him. Christ is all-inclusive with every human he created with his Spirit and likeness, and people just need to awaken to the reality of who they really are in him. When people know Christ their lives really do change for the better.

No person can deny him once they have the revelation of truth, and once that light comes on the last thing you will want to do is go back into darkness again. People say, *"Well, what about all the rebellious, evildoers and all those who betrayed Christ and hurt other people? Surely they deserve punishment in hell for all eternity."* In Scripture, we read that all sin is sin, and there is no scale of who has done greater evil works than someone who told a little white lie. If every evil person had the revelation of Christ's true love, not religion, and I'm talking about knowing him, who is grace and unconditional love, they would never intentionally kill and hurt other people. They would be healed from a false mindset and the illusion created through fear that dominated their lives. Jesus spoke to all people, to encourage them to change their minds. In Greek, the word for changing your mind is *metanoia*. Once they have the revelation of Christ's unconditional love in their hearts, it goes into their minds where it corresponds with the correct actions, causing all of society to benefit, and they stop re-offending. They have effectively been healed from a false identity and lifestyle as they have the revelation of Christ within.

The more we hate people who are doing the wrong things, the more it fuels the anger within them to carry on as the same person. I have seen criminals have the revelation of Christ's love for them, and once they see his light you won't find a more repentant and remorseful person. It is not our Father bringing on any internal punishment or condemnation, because love knows no such thing. That is the result of the sin itself, which brings with it its own punishment and the realization of what the person's actions have caused. However, the Father is right at hand to correct every person, for he is a God of relentless love, and in him there is no condemnation, only love resides. It is only through his love that people have a true corrective revelation that produces effortless change.

"So repent (change your mind and purpose); turn around and return [to God], that your sins may be erased (blotted out, wiped clean), that times of refreshing (of recovering from the effects of heat, of reviving with fresh air) may come from the presence of the Lord." Acts 3:19-21 AMPC

Sin is missing the mark, and when we look at it in terms of a relational God, it is defined by missing a relational reality; it is a distortion of the Father's image within us. It is the Greek word *"Harmartia,"* and it is made up of two words. The word *"Ha"* is a negation, like *"Un"* or *"Dis,"* and it is a negation or denial. To give you an example, it is like if you are un-coordinated; it is a denial of coordination, and if you are dis-respectful, that is a denial or a negation of respect. The word *"Martia"* comes from the Greek word *"Merros,"* which means origin or being. The word *"Harmatia"* is basically a negation or denial of your origination and of your being. Sin *"Harmitia"* is about missing the mark, but the mark is not perfect moral behavior.

The mark is the truth of your original being, or your identity as the divinity from the likeness of God of his Spirit being within you. When Adam led us towards the tree of the knowledge of good and evil, he made a way for us to follow his orders instead of God's. He showed us the wrong path, that we can operate from out of self and ego, thereby missing the mark of our original identity, which is our very origination. In effect, the fruit of missing who we really are is an isolated heart, which then creates a mind/thought separation that can lead to bad behavior. We automatically follow the path of wrong when we are not walking with Christ. As we read in Romans 3:23, ***"For all have sinned and fall short of the glory of God."*** We all decided to do what we did alone because we had a bad identity and didn't know who we were. Adam didn't separate us from God. We do not have Adam's spirit, and we're not birthed through him, but we did all make our own choice. There is no scapegoating Adam! He showed us how to remove God from our minds and follow through with our own voice and selfish ways. Jesus has undone everything for us and brought us to the tree of life, which is living from the Kingdom within; his Spirit directs us into all truth.

The wages of sin are death because anytime you operate from out of self and take the wrong path, it separates you from God in your mind. You then feel it, creating the illusion that you can't come to God; yet you can boldly come to God through Christ, who is in you. It is the separate, alone choices we make that are not in line with God's direction, which is everything that is good and beneficial for us and everyone around us. The gift of God is eternal life. Jesus has given himself to every person, and we all have the chance and opportunity to come to him and eat from the good fruit of life. He provided a way whereby we now embrace our origination and true identity and once we know our true identity, we will cease living the lie that previously held us captive.

The religious lie is that we are completely separated from God; we are born that way from birth, and we will be separated at death. It is all fear-driven and very bad news. The good news is restoration in Christ; that we all have a hope and a future in him, and we are reconciled to him. It is a restored consciousness of who we have always been. Once we believe the lie contained in the rotten fruit they feed us, the implications they lead you to are devastating. People today have totally given up on life because of the damage religion has done to them. They see grace a little, but they think they are not good enough, and there is still something they must do to get their act together before God will give them any grace. Religion sucks all the oxygen out of you, killing you with a slow damaging mind death that leads your life downhill, causing you to miss out on everything that is brilliant and inspiring in him. They believe their lives will never be good enough. They struggle to see a way out, but no matter how hard they try, they just can't seem to measure up and their deeds will never qualify them. This is the lie of works-based salvation, which is the kissing cousin of the Adamic nature lie. Both religions are based on us having to do something to qualify ourselves before we can even hope to come close to being in a relationship with God. They teach us in church all kinds of ways to fix this perceived gap of separation between you and God. They make us enroll in a five-step program if we hope to get the victory, and four steps if we want our prayers answered because he doesn't hear us. He is way up out there someplace, and we are here, so there is always this perceived separation. All of this is an absolute illusion and a totally fabricated lie.

The truth is, no humans have ever been separated from God. People throughout the Scriptures had this revelation and wrote about the all-inclusive love of God. The Spirit gives life, and apart from our Spirit we are not living on earth or eternally. Our spirit is one with our Father and the Son, and when our bodies die our spirit remains with God, and we live eternally. We all existed in God before the foundation of the world. We have his DNA and his life-giving Spirit within us as we were birthed into this world.

The very power of Jesus and the incarnation of him coming in the flesh was to unveil to those lost that we have been under a deception of separation. The human named Jesus, who walked in a body and who is God, the Christ, who is a Spirit in flesh form, came to demonstrate on behalf of all humans that there is no separation.

Do you want to know what the Father thinks about you? He thinks about you exactly as he thought about his Son.

Jesus came to show us the Father and what he thinks about us. Jesus didn't come to change God's mind; he came to change our minds about God. Jesus said, "I'm here to show you the Father's love." He embraces you just like you are without changing anything, and he has you just like you are without you having to try in your own effort to change one little bit through following rigid rules. He says to you, "You've never been separated from Me, and I love you just as you are."

I will complete this chapter with a reading from Ephesians 2:1-6 in, *"The Passion Translation."*

~ "And his fullness fills you, even though you were once like corpses, dead in your sins and offenses. It wasn't that long ago that you lived in the religion, customs, and values of this world, obeying the dark ruler of the earthly realm who fills the atmosphere with his authority, and works diligently in the hearts of those who are disobedient to the truth of God. The corruption that was in us from birth was expressed through the deeds and desires of our self-life. We lived by whatever natural cravings and thoughts our minds dictated, living as rebellious children subject to God's wrath like everyone else. But, God still loved us with such great love. He is so rich in compassion and mercy. Even when we were dead and doomed in our many sins, he united us into the very life of Christ and saved us by his wonderful grace! He raised us up with Christ the exalted One, and we ascended with him into the glorious perfection and authority of the heavenly realm, for we are now co-seated as one with Christ!"~

Chapter 5

~Religious Mind Control~

"Your sense of failure may be the catalyst God wants to use to bring you to a new understanding of the meaning of the Christian life."
Steve McVey

In general, the roots of all religion are grounded in controlling people through fear, creating mindless and obedient people. They teach us what their church believes and what their pastor says through their own ideas and theology. Religion isn't willing to let you hear from God yourself. In religion, you hear very little about the Spirit of Truth that has been given to you individually, who leads you into all truth. The teacher will tell you what they have heard from the Spirit of Truth, and then proceed to tell you what the truth is, and that you need to follow their truth the way they received it.

God never planned for it to work this way because he gave every human his Spirit of Truth within, and we do not need any man to teach us. (1 John 2:27)

Religion doesn't want to teach you how to fish and find food for yourself. It wants to give you the fish and keep you dependent because it does not want to lose control of you. I want to reassure you that it is very encouraging to have fellowship together in the body of Christ and hear from ministers who can teach us the wisdom they have learned through God. However, our own individual relationship with God will rightly discern what we are hearing from them and how to apply what is revealed for our own lives. The Christ Spirit within the speaker will resonate with the Christ Spirit within the hearer.

The apostle Paul, who is our New Testament teacher in abiding in God's unconditional love and grace, teaches people in all churches that we do not need to have a combination of Old Testament laws with New Testament grace. Paul pulls absolutely no punches, and you know our battle is not with people. It is religious laws that remove us from our relationship with God and hearing directly from him ourselves. Through their control, we are blinded. We can visualize Paul teaching the gospel of grace, and people falling head over heels in love with Jesus until the Judaizers came in and strapped on laws and regulations that people must perform to please God.

Once Paul heard about these laws and mixing it with grace, he wrote a letter to the Galatians where he explained they needed to remove all the laws and put them in their rearview mirror and never look back on it again. He expressed his concerns over having to follow any set of rules, knowing it would hinder their relationship with

Christ. Paul said to them in Galatians 3:10-14, ***"For as many as are of the works of the law are under the curse."*** And here is what the curse is, ***"For it is written cursed is everyone who does not continue in all things which are written in the book of the law, to do them. But that no one is justified by the law in the sight of God is evident, for the just shall live by faith. Yet the law is not of faith, but the man who does them shall live by them. Christ has redeemed us from the curse of the law having become a curse for us for it is written, cursed is everyone who hangs on a tree, that the blessings of Abraham might come upon the Gentiles in Christ Jesus, that we might receive the promise of the Spirit through faith."***

Religion is tied to laws and regulations, and as we read through Paul's revelation, there is no life in the law, it is dead. It's a black hole that pulls you in, and the further you get in, the deeper it drags you in, causing you to try harder to live up to what the law demands. Once you start down that road of law, it's never-ending and you have to do all of it. You can't just select a few rules and leave the rest out. This is why people burn out and give up. The pressure to fulfill it all is too impossible, causing them to live under a constant mental battle that beats them down in the end. There is nothing more electrifying than hearing Christ within speak to your spirit as you hear the living word directly for your life. Just reading words and trying to do what the rules suggest is never going to work. There is no heart relational foundation for change to genuinely take place. The Scriptures have been written by people who heard from God and were inspired to write what they heard; however, each writer is unique, having their own personalities and life trials that they shared with us. As you read their testimonies of Christ and stories, the Christ within you will illuminate what you need to hear at that time, and his words will spring to life in you where you will be able to see what God is saying to you, and the direction he wants for your life. We are all individuals and created different, there is no person who has the same life. As we read Scripture it is going to be interpreted through our own eyes and personalized with God through our relationship with him.

I've got friends, and I know people who are throwing their hands up in the air and saying, "Who needs this? I can't do it, forget it, I'm going to fail anyway." It all comes back to what teaching you are sitting under. If it's the law, it will make one of two things happen to you. Number one, you will quit and walk away upset, and when you walk away upset, you'll feel discouraged, guilty, and condemned. You'll feel worthless, you'll feel like a failure, and then wonder why everybody else can do this but you. Then number two, you'll settle for being a big hypocrite. You put on a façade, a veneer for the world to see. Outwardly you look good, but inwardly you know you just aren't cutting it.

I've done both. Often, I've looked at my life and outwardly I look pretty good, however, inwardly I knew the truth about how short I was coming. Deep down, I knew I wasn't making it. I was failing to live up to the standards of where I wanted to be. There were times and periods in my life where I just threw my hands up and said, "Who needs this" and I just walked away. I was discouraged, feeling condemned and worthless like there's no possible way I could ever do this.

"The reason religion harps on putting God above all things is because religion does not see God in all things."

Paul's theology whereby he explains God's loving grace will keep you free, and he set it out very heavily in Galatians, Ephesians, Philippians, and Colossians. It gets stronger and stronger as you really begin meditating on what he is saying and listen to the Spirit of Truth.

The book of Galatians is like Grace Teaching 101. It is going back to the basic understanding that God is love, and we don't move in him through hard cold words of laws. Instead, we connect with God through grace and in the freedom of love. I assure you that as you continue growing in unconditional love and grace, your frequency will rise higher. And as your vibration increases, each higher frequency will reveal bonds and laws that the lower frequencies couldn't recognize. Every time you elevate and move to another dimension, and another room within the house, you should become freer because you now begin seeing those little things that tried to hold on to you. I call this the undiscovered *"Ites"* such as; *Israelites, Canaanites, Hittites*. You finally arrived in the promised land, and it's remaining in the land of victory and standing firm in Christ that drives out all of your inner *"Ites."*

When you see the revelation and are still in the land of the *"Ites,"* you find yourself going back and forth in your mind, and this is our major warfare. Once you can see the new promised land, which is his refreshing revelation, if you still have your feet in the land of human made religion then your mind will go through a mental tug of war. But God is not going to stop; he will continue to reach you and take you out of the land of laws to get you to press on into his promised land. The Holy Spirit is going to bring you to a higher frequency. As he brings in new revelation, you will receive an understanding of your authentic identity. The challenge will be whether we keep moving forward or stay content where we are. We tend to stagnate and stay in one place when God has so much more that he wants to show us.

He is going to continue showing you more and more depth to what he has fully, directly, deposited into you for your life. As you grow with him and think and meditate on the things of the Spirit, as Paul said in Philippians 4:8 (emphasis added), ***"We are to think on all things that are***

good, pure, perfect, loving, and of good report." As those thoughts fill our mind our frequency elevates, and as we come to another place, we suddenly identify all those false mindsets that tried to hold us back from thinking about all those things that are good, pure, perfect, and lovely of a good report.

Sitting under religion has us feeling unworthy to be in the promised land where we can see all those things. These feelings result in our cutting ourselves off, and we live in the negative condemning land. In Galatians 3:10, Paul explains that the law produces the curse, and when you can't keep it in its entirety you are constantly in debt and hopelessly unable to see a way out. The curse from the Old Testament law that comes upon us when we live by those rules and regulations that we can't keep is threefold: poverty, sickness, and death. If you listen to the Judaizers, Paul is telling them the flow from the *"Zoe life,"* which is the God kind of life that comes through grace, will suddenly and abruptly stop flowing.

If we are to listen to the evangelical church and many other rules and law-abiding churches, we will not be any different from the Judaizers. All their laws will stop the life-giving supply to your spirit, stymying it. This is why it is so important that we continue to grow in grace. If we don't allow the grace of God to go deeper and deeper, then all humans will tend to slip back into some form of self-imposed law. That's what backsliding is. It's not falling into sin; it's falling from out of grace and going back under the laws.

When we start to see and recognize our performance, the law-abiding comes back. When this occurs, we need to immediately cut it off because, as Paul says in Galatians 5:4, we become estranged from Christ in our minds once we focus on laws. The separation in your mind becomes you attempting to justify yourself by whatever law you are using as a measuring stick to see if you are acceptable before God. When this happens, Paul explains that you have fallen from grace. That's the performance trap that grace has delivered all humans from. We don't want to ever go back to that land.

In Galatians 3:11, we read, ***"But that no one is justified by the law in the sight of God is evident, for the just shall live by faith."*** So, what is justification exactly? Justification is setting you in a position just as if you had never sinned, and he said this does not come by the law; it comes by the hearing of faith. Whose faith does Scripture refer to? It is not your faith, your priest's faith, or your pastor's faith. It comes by your trust in his faith, and that's what justifies you. Faith is you hearing from God yourself for your own individual life, which is your personal relationship with him. Be careful not to make faith a major work, for that's one of the pitfalls you're going to face if you don't keep growing in grace. We attempt to exercise our faith by our actions, when in fact, faith comes by hearing and hearing by the word of God. (Romans 10:17)

The word of God *is* Christ *in* you. He is the living word of God who reveals all truth to you, and it's not just words on paper.

"So faith comes by hearing [what is told], and what is heard comes by the preaching of the message that came from the lips] of Christ (the Messiah himself)."
Romans 10:17 AMPC

In most cases, we have been taught that the more we read our Bible the stronger our faith will become or, the more Scriptures we confess, and all the activities we do will build our faith. We thought that if we just confessed and memorized Scripture, along with daily meditation, that this is faith when doing all these things can often be a work. Reading Scripture is beneficial, and so is meditating on Scripture. However, we then rest after reading inspired words and allow the Spirit within to rise up and reveal truths. This is when we hear from God for our own personal lives. Faith comes when you hear what God has said to you personally, then you will enter his perfect rest. Have you ever tried to make a decision while under anxiety and stress? If so, you know how difficult it can be to discern the right way to go when there is a heavy burden on your shoulders. We cannot force hearing from God and what he wants to reveal to us when we are under pressure, because our minds will not readily accept truths while in a state of anxiety and fear. It is possible to have a burden while remaining sound minded and in control so you can hear from God for the right outcome, and his comfort. We read this throughout Scripture in the godly lives of people under extreme duress. We rest and enjoy fellowship with Christ, and as we rest, we can easily hear his direction.

When you hear from God it is clear, and you haven't tried to build any kind of faith yourself. It is a natural conversation with God about your life. It is trusting what you hear from God and what he has already done and knows will be the most beneficial way for you to move. A good example is being a parent or even a guardian. If you have a good amount of life experience, you can see the road ahead and know the right direction the person under your charge needs to take. You know the pain and struggles of life, and you can effectively discern and suggest a more profitable way to go that will benefit them. God is the same with his children. He has done everything. It is finished, and now it is up to us to hear his correct guidance for our life. God gives every human free will to decide which way to go, and with all your good intentions and suggestions, the decision remains up to you which land to occupy. When you are inspired by the word God has spoken to you and it resonates within, go in that direction no matter what your eyes see in the natural. We often hear God but then think, *"No I will go this other way."* and then something happens to where it didn't work out. Then there are times we heard God and went his way and still something happened. However, instead of standing in what God said and talking to him about the situation, we got upset and tried to correct what we did by going another way that we thought will *"Fix the problem."* God's direction is always right for us; when we take his path, it will often encounter hurdles but that doesn't mean you heard wrong from God. It means that every path we take will have other people, and not all of them are walking with God or even know God, so there are going to be challenges. But as we listen to God, we will overcome them. You are always hearing right and moving in the right direction anytime it has its foundation in love. Love always wins, and God is only going to direct you through love which produces the right outcome in all situations.

When God speaks in your spirit, you're going to be energized by what he says to you and directly deposits in your spirit, and that is his faith. I might share a word that will charge your spirit in his faith, but it was not because of my faith. It is the Christ Spirit within you who fuels what you heard and inspires you in him. Faith is not this thing you try to build up within yourself until one day you wake up and become a faith giant, and then set out to believe and receive all the material things you desire along with successful titles; all in a vain attempt to make you feel you are now in God's good books. This is not what faith is at all. Once you understand what he has done through believing, receiving becomes easy with no effort whatsoever. You will take what he gives you without having to do anything at all. It will be a natural spiritual flow in your life, and you will respond to what God says to you. It becomes a genuine change of mind out of love, not a law that you need to confess before God and say, *"I repent,"* for that action happens as you hear the truth. It becomes a relational acceptance so that, as you hear God, you change your mind from the futility of what you tried to develop yourself.

The apostle Paul penned some tremendous revelations on God's unconditional love and how to walk with him in grace. However, one of the most outstanding books he wrote that shows our liberty and freedom from religion is Galatians. Paul dedicates his epistle to helping them be released from the clutches of religion. He talks about the pullback into religion and what often happens when we encounter the gospel.

Jesus often talked in parables that bypassed the mind and knowledge of all the laws embodied in religion. He spoke directly into people's spirits. The religious people could not perceive what he was saying because their moral blindness prevented them from hearing. He said in Matthew 13:13, ***"Therefore I speak to them in parables,***

because seeing they do not see, and hearing they do not hear, nor do they understand." Jesus came to abolish working for the law, to try to perform from an attitude of having to obey rules. He came to demonstrate the Father and how to live in a relationship with the Father, and by doing so, he enabled us to now fulfill all the laws naturally through love.

In Galatians 4:21-31 (emphasis added), Paul had to convince them of their legalistic ways and that they had turned back into error. He said, ***"Tell me you who desire to be under the law do you not hear the law?"*** In other words, do you understand what the law entails? You are wanting to be under rules and regulations rather than hearing from God yourself. In Galatians 4:22, he continues to say, ***"For it is written that Abraham had two sons: the one by a bondwoman the other by a freewoman."*** He's going to start drawing analogies to law and grace, freedom, and bondage between Abraham's work with a handmaiden, Hagar, and his wife, Sarah.

Paul continues in Galatians 4:23 and said, ***"But he who was of the bondwoman was born according to the flesh and he of the freewoman through promise which things are symbolic."*** Paul is speaking symbolically here to represent an important change. Then he says, ***"For these are the two covenants: the one from Mount Sinai which gives birth to bondage, which is Hagar the handmaiden. For this Hagar is Mount Sinai in Arabia and corresponds***

to Jerusalem which now is in bondage with her children." Jerusalem is, of course, the center of the Jewish religion. He's explaining to the people that he's making a symbolic teaching. Paul was teaching them metaphorically, likening the law to Jerusalem and to Hagar, which is a picture of religion with its bondage. Paul continues to stress his point in Galatians 4:26-29 (emphasis added), ***"But the Jerusalem that is from up above is free which is the mother of us all, and gave birth to us all. He said; rejoice O barren, you who do not bear and break forth and shout, you who are not in labor, for the desolate has many more children than she who has a husband. Now we brethren as Isaac was are children of promise but he who was born according to the flesh persecuted him who was born according to the Spirit, even so it is now."***

Paul points out a true statement; that those born and brought up under the law are always the ones persecuting those who are in liberty or from the promise. They are totally void of any form of a relationship with God, being unable to see past their own self-righteous works.

Today, we see this with religion persecuting those of us who are walking in the liberty of grace, and this is what Paul is addressing.

In Galatians 4:30, (paraphrased) Paul continues, ***"Nevertheless, what does the Scripture say? Cast out the bondwoman and her son, cast out the law of bondage and because they should not be an heir with the son of the***

freewoman, so then brethren we are not children of the bondwoman we are children of the free."

When you are reading through these verses, if you don't understand where Paul is coming from it can sound confusing, especially if you are coming out of religion. He is making an analogy between law and grace, between freedom and bondage, between flesh and Spirit, between religion and the gospel, and he does so by setting up this dualistic comparison.

Paul uses Hagar and Ishmael as a type of the law and the flesh's activity to accomplish what God gave by his promise. Remember the story of Abraham and Sarah? God promised them in their old age, which was well up into their 90s, that they would have a child. But when Sarah heard that promise, she actually laughed. She knew she was past childbearing age, but God made them a promise, just as he does with us through our relationship with him. When God gave them a promise and when he gives us a promise, we don't always see it for some time. As time goes along, what often happens when we don't seem to acquire what God told us we are to have, we try to achieve the goal by the flesh, which is alone and separated from God in our own efforts.

That's what Abraham did but Sarah came up with her own idea of how to accomplish what God told her she would have. She said (paraphrasing), ***"Look why don't you take my handmaiden Hagar? She is a young woman and***

she can bear the child." Abraham thought that was a great idea, so off he went and bore a child named Ishmael with Hagar. Paul's analogy likens Ishmael to what happens when we try to do something in our flesh. I know there have been times in my life where I stepped out ahead of God, and it never went very well. Yet God, in all his mercy, will always help us turn around and heed his direction. He will restore all our errors, but it's like a very big detour that we didn't have to take if we had just waited on his timing. Have you ever had any Ishmael's in your life? God promised you something, but you grew weary waiting for the completion of the promise, so you set out to accomplish it yourself. What you produce in your fleshly efforts is called Ishmael, which are those things that you try diligently to do in your own strength through trying to help God out. It is because we have grown impatient and don't trust God to really follow through on his promise. Then, once we have tried everything and find out that it wasn't such a great idea after all to go down that road and try to do what only God can do, we finally throw our hands up and say, *"God, help me get out of this mess."*

Of course, God will help you get out of that mess. He will not leave you stranded, but now there may be more waiting to undo what you have created. Trusting God and having patience is the key throughout your life walk with God. There is no point in going out ahead of him because he is the one who knows what things lie ahead and why you have to go at the pace you are going.

He knows why it needs to take that long, and it has nothing to do with delaying you or wanting you to wait while he sits back laughing. He tells us in Habakkuk 2:3, ***"For the vision is yet for an appointed time; But at the end it will speak, and it will not lie. Though it tarries, wait for it; Because it will surely come, it will not tarry."***

The best thing you can do is to stay in your relationship with him. When temptation comes and you are considering wandering off in your own direction, perhaps think of Abraham and Sarah when they did the same thing you are about to do. It didn't turn out too good. It created more drama in their lives than if they had waited on God to do what he said he would do. Religion will always have you running around doing everything in your own strength aside from him, causing a great deal of anxiety and frustration.

Paul is using Hagar and Ishmael as a type of the law and flesh activities we enter into to try and accomplish what God has given us by promise, which was the promised son Isaac through Sarah. This eventually happened even though they were approaching 100 years old.

"Religion sees the death of one man on the cross, the Father sees the death of all men. Religion sees the resurrection of one man, the Father sees the resurrection and birth of all men from death to new life."

I want to bring out the context of their situation and bring it into today's reality to ensure you live free through his grace and liberty, no longer having anymore Hagar religious entanglements. All you need to do is hear him and step out in that direction. You will know when you hear him because your spirit will rise within you as God makes it clear what he wants you to do. In religion, there is no relationship with God, resulting in people stepping out in their own desires that are often contrary to God's desires because they do not know him.

Ishmael's always produce less than God's best. God has promised us, just as God promised Abraham, but if we try to gain the promise through our flesh actions, we produce what Abraham produced, an Ishmael. When we do this, we fail to receive the right promise, the Isaac, the son of promise, and we don't get the very best that God has for us. Here's the bottom line; *you can never produce by the flesh what was promised by the Spirit, no matter how hard you try.*

I want to help you understand your freedom in Christ and move you away from the oppression separation causes. I want you to be free, no longer being in bondage to those things that might still be clinging to your life. God has given you and me a promise, just as he did to Abraham. If we try to fulfill the promise of salvation God has given us, of wholeness, of liberty, of freedom, everything that Jesus provided for us through the finished work of the cross; if we try to perform that by flesh activity, we will only produce what Abraham produced, which is an Ishmael. When you walk in a relationship with Christ through everything he has done, he will be your light unto your feet. Even when you walk in dark valleys, he is with you and will protect you. We read his promises right through the Bible, and you would personally be hearing from him regarding your own life and what he promised you. In Psalm 32:8, he tells us through David, ***"I will instruct you and teach you in the way you should go, I will guide you with my eye."***

Be encouraged today to continue in your own personal journey in faith with Christ within. Hear him, rest in knowing that what he promised you will be fulfilled in his perfect timing.

We will end this chapter with a message from Steve McVey from his book; *"Grace Walk."*

"So many Christians today measure the success of their spiritual lives by whether they live up to religious rules. They focus on their performance. They try to live up to the standard they have set for themselves, but they can never do enough. No wonder they feel defeated! Your sense of failure may be the catalyst God wants to use to bring you to a new understanding of the meaning of the Christian life. When Christians try to live by rules, the outcome will be the same as it has always been. They will discover that they just can't measure up, regardless of how hard they try. The law is intended to make people realize; I just can't do it. I've tried and tried, but I just can't live a successful Christian life. If that's how you feel, then you might be closer than you know to enjoying success. Your sense of failure may be the catalyst God wants to use to bring you to a new understanding of the meaning of the Christian life."

Chapter 6

~Sin Consciousness~

"Separation from the source of existence, means non-existence. It is impossible to be separated from God and remain alive."
Mo Thomas

We previously discussed how we can create Ishmaels in our lives through the works of our flesh. We also emphasized that Paul taught us about the freedom from the law you have when you are in Christ. Religion focuses on the law and words on paper, and then doing your best to obey them, thinking that by doing so you would please God. We know that real pleasing God occurs when we are in a relationship with him, and he is our life and focus, not cold words on paper. His Spirit is life, and the words by themselves can do nothing.

We have been working our way through the various religious entanglements that may still have a hold on us as we progress in grace. We must recognize these little dogs that nip at our heels as they try to pull us back into some form of religious bondage. Paul talked about becoming free from religion, and the best thing to do is to make sure that all bonds and chains, cords, and ties we still may have are removed.

Have you noticed how religion tries to get you to a place of victory? The gospel of grace that Paul taught isn't trying to get us to a place of victory, it's teaching us to live from that place of victory. Religion tries to get us to a place of victory by our sacrifice, our diligence, and our discipline so that God will bless us with a victorious lifestyle. Paul had the revelation that we are already in that place of victory, and it is through this realization and a change of mind that we can begin living from that place.

How can you tell if religion still has a grip on your life? I will help you distinguish this so you can remove all the barriers and start walking with Christ and be free in your mind.

If you still have ties to religion, you will never be 100% sure that you are 100% forgiven. You will constantly have this feeling of uncertainty, and this is the hold religion has to keep your mind going around and around again.

As I talk with a lot of people who are just coming into the liberty and grace of Christ within, I find the thing that holds people in check is their having a sin consciousness. They are absolutely not sure if they are saved and are one with Christ, no matter what they have done to try and win his acceptance. They are not sure they're completely forgiven because a little taint of sin consciousnesses seeks to bind them. The root of feeling unforgiven by God is the constant programming that you are a sinner in the eyes of God, and you have an Adamic separate nature that is not of God. You have been so built up and had this human-made instruction for so long it has become locked in your heart. It is a constant thought that you have to do something and make some kind of sacrifice to be forgiven. It has become really hard for you to see that forgiveness is a gift from God through Christ Jesus, who has done everything on your behalf. I understand how hard it is to remove all the built-up garbage that continues clouding your mind; many of us have come through the same doors you went through. I can assure you, through the Christ Spirit that is within you, all the chains are smashing off you now, and your liberty is only a thought away. He is in you, and he has done it all, and receiving everything he has for you is only a matter of taking the key in your hand, who is Christ, and let him unlock the prison doors of your mind.

"The Place where you are experiencing what religion taught you is warfare, in reality it is great insight into where you need to renew your mind to your authentic identity as divinity."

Religion has you bound up, thinking that you have so much sin in your life that no matter how hard you try, sin just keeps on reproducing itself in you again and again. It is a feeling that you have some sort of limited timeframe of forgiveness, and if you take that one sin too far then that's it, it's all over; there is no more forgiveness for you. Let me help you, my friend. You can never out sin God's love, mercy, and forgiveness. The only reason you might still be entertaining a sin consciousness and repeating the same errors is through a faulty belief system. You've had the bondage doctrine tied to you, never realizing that you don't need all of that rubbish. A relationship you have with Christ releases all the power of darkness; and through his love you will automatically know you are always forgiven, always loved. You are whole, and just as he is, you are in this world. Once you start walking with him, you will learn the right steps to take, and your whole life will start to change effortlessly.

This brings me to the next critical topic, which is the unpardonable sin. I really need to do a little explaining here to help you understand what this is and set your mind free. I can't tell you how many people I have spoken to who have been terrorized by thinking they have committed the unpardonable sin. Let me assure you that you have not committed the unpardonable sin.

In Matthew 12:31, Jesus says, ***"Therefore I say to you, every sin and blasphemy will be forgiven men, but the blasphemy against the Spirit will not be forgiven men."*** Religion likes to twist this Scripture; however, notice that Jesus was speaking to the Pharisees, and warning them. God can forgive every human so far as every human believes in Christ and everything he has done for us. How can God forgive anyone if people don't first believe in Jesus Christ? God has forgiven every human, but not every human believes, so they can't enter what he has provided for us, which is his forgiveness, and an abundant life because of their own rebellion against Christ. The Pharisees refused to see the Father in Christ no matter how much he demonstrated the Father right before their very eyes. The Father is waiting to take them all with open arms. Forgiveness is done, healing is for everyone today, but if you are against the Spirit within, then the suffering is because of you, not because of God. The Kingdom within you is the opposite of the way this world sees things. Healing is your true identity; sickness in all its forms is a lie. All that is required for humanity to do is correct our vision. Clean the glass and see who Christ says we are, and then we will have everything he says we have. The miracles that we think are a phenomenon are, in truth, our reality. If we believe in sickness, lack, and poverty, then that is believing a lie, and it is a matter of changing our mind to his truth.

The fact that you have ever worried about this Scripture and been so scared that maybe you have done something wrong towards God, and now he cannot forgive you shows you straight away that you believe. You love God, you love Christ, and you want to please him. Even if you have come under the bondage of religion and believe in Christ, you are fully forgiven. Unfortunately, to those who don't believe, God can't help them until they come to him, but he will never give up or stop trying to reach them. He wants you spared from your own mental suffering. Everything God does, he does for all humanity. He is not a tormentor, and there is no part of evil whatsoever in our loving Father.

This whole idea of sin consciousness that religion has created and failed to tell you was that the Father does not deal in forgiveness through installments! We've all come through that feeling where we believe the only time God forgave our sin is when we asked him to. Therefore, he forgives in installments, so to speak. When you asked, he forgave. If you didn't ask, then there was no forgiveness. You receive forgiveness here and there depending on your asking him to forgive you for those sins you can think of at that moment. But what about all the things you can't remember? What if you weren't sorry enough? What if you didn't repent in sackcloth, ashes and tears? What if you didn't show enough remorse? What religion fails to tell you is that God doesn't forgive in increments. The Father doesn't do forgiveness just a little bit at a time. In fact, he has taken care of the sin problem, which to God does not exist. He has forgiven all sins past, present, and future, and they are all done away with forever.

"And coming out of the graves after his resurrection, they went into the holy city and appeared to many." Matthew 27:53

John the Baptist recognized all forgiveness when he first saw Jesus in John 1:29. He pointed to Jesus and said, ***"Behold! The lamb of God who takes away the sin of the world."*** The sin is singular; *the sin of the world.* The sin the religious church calls the Adamic nature, that you are separated from God. Although that phrase is never used in Scripture, that's a human-made doctrine, John looks at Jesus and realized the sin problem would be taken care of through Jesus. Sin, at that time before Jesus had resurrected and ascended, was that man had separated himself from having a relationship with God. Christ was perfect in all that he did, and he walked in a total relationship with the Father and only did what he saw the Father do. We read in Matthew 27:53 that when Christ resurrected, his Spirit entered all previous humans who were dead, and they came out of their tombs and walked in the streets. His Spirit entered all those who were alive and walking that day, and his Spirit is in every human that will ever be born in the future. The sin and forgiveness problem is solved and done away with. You have the Christ Spirit within you, and that can never be taken out or away from you, so be totally at ease in knowing that you are sealed, redeemed, and bought with a price. You can never not be forgiven.

I want you to have full reassurance in your mind that sin is not an issue in your life. In Colossians 2:13 (paraphrased), Paul said, ***"And you being dead in your trespasses and the uncircumcision of your flesh in that condition,*** and the last part of that verse says, ***he made alive together with him having forgiven you all your trespasses."***

You were in that dead trespass condition, and now he has forgiven you all your trespasses by making you alive together in him. There is no sin, no trespass, no transgression that has a hold on you that brings death. All humans are forgiven, although not everyone will believe; therefore, they stay in darkness but that does not change that it is finished. There is no longer any sin, it is humans who alienated themselves in their minds, living the life of the Old Testament through the door of mind separation that Adam opened. Do you see the hunger and the heart of Paul, and how he wanted so desperately to let everyone know that they are forgiven and have the Spirit of Christ within them? Nobody has to remain in darkness. Paul was so passionate because of his own experience with Christ's love that he wanted to go to any extreme to reach people and share this good news.

"He then would have had to suffer often since the foundation of the world, but now once at the end of the

ages he has appeared to put away sin, by the sacrifice of himself." Hebrews 9:26

I'm going to put a caveat in here because every time I teach on this subject of the freedom we have in Christ people get the idea that this means you can do anything you want. The religious people like to say that what I am teaching means everyone can go and do anything they want because God is not going to judge anyone, as all sin is done away with and gone.

We read in Romans 6:23, ***"For the wages of sin is death."*** What judges you is the sin. It is the thing you did that was not in line with your walk with God. You are not found guilty, and you're not judged for your sin by God. What you feel is you being judged by your own sin. The wages of sin is death, but it's not a judgment from God. Sin, which is an error, a wrong action, is going to produce a death inside of you because you will become aware in your spirit that you did something from out of yourself, and this thing was not an action you did that was in line with your relationship with God. It is an error that has come from out of the sin or the dilemma. Here is an example. If you rob a bank, God is not putting that on your record. But just because God has already forgiven you for robbing the bank that doesn't mean you will not go to prison for ten years. There is still a kickback to the transgression and wrong thought that produced the wrong action, but it didn't come from God. You automatically know when you are thinking and doing things that are not in line with God's best for you. We have what is right and what is wrong written in our hearts. We know, yet sometimes fail to follow God through life situations. Then we can get into all kinds of errors and troubles that we brought upon ourselves, and in that, we can feel our own punishment. That chastisement is not from God. If you rob a bank and find yourself in jail, you can still turn to God and be in a relationship with him. That is what he wants, and then through God's love and as you walk with him and learn of him, you are not likely to go down that same rotten path again. You might even get out of jail earlier and turn your life around, then help other people turn their lives around. It is not the end because anyone has stepped out in error, no matter what that error of judgment and mind separation caused.

Jesus spoke of this in Luke 7:47 when the Pharisees questioned Jesus regarding the manner of the woman pouring out a valuable perfume to demonstrate her love for Jesus, ***"Therefore I say to you, her sins, which are many, are forgiven for she loved much. But to whom little is forgiven, the same loves little."*** This woman was repentant, she recognized God's love, and she came to him just as she was, and he fully accepted her. People who live a wrong life have within themselves the hardest penalty of all once the truth is revealed to them. They are incredibly sorry, and when love hits a former hard heart, the harsh reality is going to be a fully regretful and remorseful person. At times, a person can feel unforgiven because they now see the harsh reality of what they have done, but the truth is they are completely forgiven, and there is no need for them to go back in their mind and relive the moment. What is necessary is to only move forward in him. Imagine if the apostle Paul, who was once a religious leader who killed Christians, came to the reality of Christ's love yet remained in the mindset of going back and dwelling on what he'd done wrong. I believe that is why he said we must press on and go forward because there is no value in looking back. It is walking out your life now, today, in Christ at this very moment and what lies ahead, keeping your mind fixed on him as you move forward.

God's love wins all the time. He will reach anyone, no matter how far they have fallen or what they have done. God wants everyone free and to know the truth that Christ is in them, and they can live their best life ever. We don't need religious laws and rules, it is the freedom found in love that sets every single person at liberty, without exception.

It is because of God's power of complete love and forgiveness for every human that he raised us up in Christ Jesus to receive the full blessings of life eternally, and to live in the heavenly realm right now. We don't need to wait. We can live in his Kingdom from this moment forward and see all things through his eternal eyes of love.

We were once dead, but that has long been changed through Christ, who has given us the living hope that all things are possible through he who resides in us.

I will finish this chapter with an inspiring insight into the Father's love from Natasha Trezebiatowski's encounter with his all-consuming fire of Love, from her testimony, from Debauchery to Christ.

~ ***"I had awakened to Christ within me. I was absorbed in his deep abundant Love. It is a Love so deep, passionate, indescribable, and individually unique to each of us in our experience with him. No time existed, only Love. I saw fire as I gazed up as I was immersed in the most consuming passion of Love that any human could ever understand, it surpassed all knowledge, and it's measure too deep and too wide. Too extraordinary for any words to capture his incredible dynamic Love. His all-consuming passion of intoxicating Love burned up any anxiety, depression, and trauma which all have its roots in fear. He replaced the old fearful religious me, and he delighted me in his brilliant judgment of pure divine unconditional Love.***

Being In Love is complete fulfillment, it is a marriage union where his divine unconditional Love never fails." ~

1 Corinthians 13:8

https://www.godnoreligion.com/

Chapter 7

~The Deadly Mix~

"The difference between what the church and Paul teach is simply this...The church shows Christ to you, but Paul reveals Christ in you."
Don Keathley

Religious teachings are very much like a game of chance because you never know if God is going to bless your situation or not. It depends on you, and whether you are demonstrating the right level of faith to receive the desired outcome. It teaches that if we obey and believe in the grace of obedience to do good works for God, then not only are we assured safety from hell, we will also reap the blessings from God in our life. If we obey the written letter and do our best, maybe we can squeeze just enough faith from our own belief to get that prayer answered. If your faith wasn't strong enough, then the pressure is on you to try even harder. Perhaps, upon not receiving your prayer, you may go back to some Old Testament Scriptures on obedience and sacrifice and then mix it with some New

Testament grace and love to see what kind of mixed formula you will create to produce the results you want.

It's no wonder people are so confused and disillusioned in the church, causing them to leave by the masses. Living our lives under a mixed message of grace and works will always produce fear, anxiety, insecurity, and uncertainty. The religious church body taught us to try and win Christ over by mixing a little bit of sacrifice with obedience, and then attach to it some kind of unmerited favor that the church calls grace or faith. If we do all this and get it right, then things might just work out for us. However, there is a *but.* And the but is that it never worked out for anyone who blends this toxic brew together. It was never meant or intended to be a formula in this way. If we don't see the Father through the person of Jesus Christ and everything he has done for us, then it is not a real picture of our loving Father.

Religion has a sibling, which is the mixed message of the Old Testament laws and the New Testament grace teachings through the Christian faith. These teachings are widely disseminated around the world through televangelists and in your local church. You're going to find that the most popular Christian teachings will offer you the mixed platter of good and bad fruit no matter what denomination you attend.

Paul is our New Testament grace teacher and theologian, and he pioneered the right way in which we were all to go since the resurrection and ascension of Christ, which is when we all received the Holy Spirit. In the book of Galatians, we read Paul's heart in disputing the teachings of the law that had crept back into the church, along with a sprinkle of grace. He focused on correcting people to see Christ through the eyes of grace and unconditional love.

Paul was the one who opened their eyes up to the love of Christ within and the grace message. After he left, some religious people came in who were Jewish believers. They believed in Jesus and grace; however, they also believed they needed to keep the law and all the ceremonies. Many of these Jewish traditions are widely seen in the church to this day. I have personally never been drawn to the Jewishness of Christianity. I know some people try to keep the feasts and meals, and all of that is fine if that is what lights your fire!

Paul explains to us in Colossians 2:16-17, ***"So let no one judge you in food or in drink, or regarding a festival, or a new moon or sabbaths, which are a shadow of things to come, but the substance is of Christ."***

Our reality is in Christ, and this is who we are. It is not about following all the rituals and formulas. These no longer have any bearing or substance on us because we now have Christ in us, the hope of glory. (Colossians 1:27) Christ is the end of the law, and this is the very message and heart of what Paul was trying to get across to everyone.

Paul was dealing with people within the church who had a religious attitude to the simplicity of the grace message. Paul writes to us in the book of Galatians, which is a tremendous guide to freedom, about the liberty we have in Christ. Paul was bringing people back to the place of authenticity we had from the very beginning of the foundation of the world.

Paul sets Jesus right on center stage, which is; Jesus plus nothing else. Not Jesus plus circumcision, not Jesus plus the ten commandments, not Jesus plus the laws of the Baptist church, the Catholic Church, the Lutheran Church, or any other denomination trying to present Christ through laws. Paul set's Christ right on center stage as the source, as our sustainer and the finisher of our Salvation.

There are a lot of mixtures in the church that the Spirit of Truth is currently weeding out because they are just like religion. It is still teaching people that they need to do certain things to be right with God. Especially if your church is preaching grace and then holding celebrations with special ceremonial days. This can be very confusing. Paul is telling everyone that we do not need to add to our faith, and our belief, or our confessions, nor our actions. There is nothing that we can add to what Christ has already done for us.

The Galatians had gone back to obeying certain religious requirements, and when we go back to laws it perverts the gospel, and we distort it. We have not seen

Christ correctly; these religious requirements block us from obtaining a clear vision of him and unconditional love. Many of us go back to adding in some conditions because it's hard on our religious minds, since we have some very deeply entrenched ideas about what we have to do and should not do to be a good Christian. Paul systemically debunks all of that, bringing liberation and freedom to trust in Jesus' faith, his obedience, and his finished work as ours. He is my obedience. I am no longer striving to be obedient; I am obedient in agreement with Christ. I'm not looking for ways to die and crucify my flesh because my old man was crucified with Christ.

"It is no longer I who live but Christ who lives in me." (Galatians 2:20)

We've picked up in religion and churches a lot of this stuff that has been added to the gospel by making us think we have to "*Do*" certain things when instead, we just need to "*Be.*" What we believe we have to do to arise and become to be accepted by Christ, Paul debunks.

Paul had a tremendous revelation of Christ, who is God in human form. He personally saw and had the revelation of God's unconditional love that was fully demonstrated through Christ. Paul was not going to move off the gospel that he received from Christ; he couldn't because he had seen the truth in the person of Christ. Paul had a transformative encounter with Christ and the complete revelation of who he is in him. This revelation was not written in any book. Paul first experienced him and then documented all his encounters, which comprise the teachings we read today.

Like so many throughout the Bible, Paul teaches us that Christ is personalized in our own individual lives and not through a book. The Bible is an incredible source of wisdom, and it is beneficial and inspiring to read and hear Christ speak to us. The words come alive in your spirit, and as you read the light comes on, and you receive the revelation that corresponds in your life. Then once you encounter and experience him, you can see the truth and then automatically your life changes. Paul came from a place of religion to revelation, and I think that we can all relate to this on some level.

In Galatians 1:11-12, we can hear Paul's heart as he states that everything he was teaching came straight from the Spirit of Truth himself, which he encountered. Paul was not teaching through any laws and rules that he read on paper as he explains in Galatians 1:11-12.

"But I make known to you brethren, that the gospel which was preached by me is not according to man. For I neither received it from man nor was I taught it, but it came through the revelation of Jesus Christ."

Paul had come from a Judaism background. He was well educated, and he was persecuting the church of God beyond measure through cold hard laws that were infused in his heart. (Galatians 1:13) He continues on to say in verse 14, ***"And I advanced in Judaism beyond many of my contemporaries in my own nation being more exceedingly zealous for the traditions of my fathers."*** The apostle Paul was the consummate master in the traditions of religion! Paul was totally enthralled with a zealous feeling that he was doing God's work by destroying the church, capturing Christians, and even murdering people through his religious mindset. At that point, Paul did not have a personal relationship through his spirit with God, for he was going by cold human-made doctrines and rules that had no life or heartbeat in them.

However, God was pursuing Paul just as he does with all humans, and there was timing to the day that Paul would meet Christ head-on, and the Father's love was revealed in him. In Galatians 1:15-17, Paul tells us, ***"But when it pleased God, who separated me from my mother's womb and called me through his grace to reveal his Son in me that I might preach him among the Gentiles, I did not immediately confer with flesh and blood nor did I go up to Jerusalem to those that were apostles before me, but I went to Arabia and returned again to Damascus."*** It was through his revelation of the overwhelming love that God has for him in Christ and for all humanity that transformed him. Paul was instantly transported from out of cold lifeless laws and into God's dynamic love. Now, Paul was immersed into a relationship with Christ within and he became very bad news to the legalistic cold churches that were loveless!

Paul gives us a brief insight into his personal life journey from being deeply entrenched in Judaism, and how he came out of it and into the revelation that Jesus hand-picked and delivered Paul to himself. He's talking about a journey from bondage to freedom, and then in Galatians 1:18-24, Paul assures us that everything he tells us is not a lie. He continues his journey to reveal Christ, with many people marveling because he was the man who persecuted the church with an unrivalled zeal.

Being a master religious teacher, Paul knew exactly what being entrenched in religion produced in life, bondage. He explained to people that the gospel he preached did not come to him according to his human-made traditions as a Judaizer. (Galatians 1:11) He explained in Galatians 1:12, ***"For I neither received it from man, nor was I taught it, but it came through the revelation of Jesus Christ."*** What gives us all boldness and confidence to proclaim the truth is when we have the revelation of Christ in us. We come alive in our spirit with his Spirit and not through laws and rules. When revelation comes and brings light to your spirit, it carries the message of truth in grace. Nobody can take that away from you once you have experienced him. Paul was powerfully bold, he knew what had come to him was directly deposited into his spirit by Jesus Christ, and it was not something he was taught in Seminary.

His revelation wasn't handed down to him through a conference or a Sunday morning church service. He got it from the Spirit of God; he received it straight from Jesus, and when he turns on the light, you won't help but be confident in your proclamations. It doesn't make you haughty or arrogant, instead it feeds humility. It is religion that puffs us up. We build ourselves up on all our degrees and what we know, but they are only words and head knowledge, and in that alone, there is no life. When I look back on everything I have learned in the last 16 years, it doesn't make me proud or arrogant. Instead, it tells me that I couldn't have gotten what I have through my intellect, my cleverness, or my ability to connect the dots or do all the things you normally would do to come to an understanding of this powerful message. My stability comes from knowing Christ and through the revelations I receive from him. When what you see is taught to you by man, it enters your head, your soul, and it lacks this spirit punch that revelation carries. More than anything, we are first in a relationship with him, and then everything else from him will come pouring out of us, which will be what is right and profitable and for everyone.

Revelation carries an electric power charge which radiates through your whole body, putting you on a different frequency which resonates with your inner spirit.

Then it becomes yours, and nobody can take away what he has revealed to you. We can receive revelation through all kinds of ways, and it can work in combination through listening to other people teach you. Sometimes I will listen to a grace teacher, a finished works teacher who will teach something that will then spur me over to where the Spirit of God shows me. There are times I read a book and it resonates in my spirit, then all of a sudden, I see something that I may not have seen before. That's the way the Spirit of God works; that's the way revelation comes. It's not the words that give you your life; it is Christ Spirit within who is speaking to you when you are reading or listening to the radio, television, and all means through life. God can reach you right where you are at, and it's up to us to have our receiving ears tuned in to listen. Everything God is teaching and showing you is for YOU! He wants you to have a personal relationship with him and to encounter life with him.

"The world is full of so-called prayer warriors, who are prayer ignorant. They're full of formulas and programs and advice, peddling techniques for getting what you want from God. Don't fall for that nonsense. This is your Father you are dealing with, and he knows better than you what you need."

Matthew 6:7 The Message Bible

Revelation is not an intellectual assent. It's not mental assent, and it's not something that you can say, *"I've got my head around it, and I think I get it now."* No. It will resonate in your spirit, and it becomes you. Religion will make you a parrot, where you repeat everything you've learned and have been taught. It is cold hard words that bear nothing in your spirit. It only sticks to your brain where you are puffed up on your own self-induced knowledge.

The miraculous trumpet of revelation will sound a blast through you, and then you won't be able to help but share this amazing healthy fruit for all to hear, then the level of frequency you hover on will affect and resonate with people. Paul was facing all kinds of adversaries, but he got his strength, courage, and boldness directly from Christ, who empowered him to go out and share this marvelous truth to all people. Paul is really transparent with the Galatian people, and he openly admits he was full of dead works and puffed up with education, causing him to have misguided priorities.

I will add that I am not in any way against going to a Bible College or obtaining degrees and education. We can all learn in various ways and grow in Christ through our relationship with him. However, religious knowledge can puff us up and stipulate that we need to do certain things. So, we need to remain humble and teachable through the Spirit of Truth, who guides us.

Through his strict religious works, Paul could see that he was not in line with the truth of who God is. As such, he needed to see and meet unconditional love and then move away from the clutches of cold hard religion, which misguides our priorities in our religious mind. It carries the deception that you are pleasing God somehow, which is where all the knowledge and self-good works can puff us up. Paul thought he was doing God a service when he persecuted the church and killed Christians. He tried to wipe the church off the face of the earth and thought he was doing God a favor, and this created an enormous zeal in him. His enthusiasm was built upon himself, not on the rock of Christ. He carried the mind deception that what he was doing was pleasing God, which created some excitement. Religious traditions always try to *"Snuff out"* what it doesn't agree with and isn't in line with its own rule-keeping. In Colossians chapter 2:6-7, Paul says, ***"As you therefore have received Christ Jesus the Lord, to walk in him, rooted and built up in him and established in the faith, as you have been taught, abounding in it with thanksgiving."*** Paul then proceeds to explain to us in verse 8, ***"Beware lest anyone cheat you through philosophy and empty deceit, according to the tradition of men, according to the basic principles of the world, and not according to Christ."***

It's amazing how zealous and enthused religious people can become while they carry a deception that they're doing

God a favor. As Paul explains, it is through their philosophy and traditions that they try to negate the life of excitement you have in Christ.

Here is something that I want you to understand about religious people: *The greatest threat to whatever God is doing today are those who were a part of what God did yesterday but refuse to move to what he's doing today.* Many people remain stuck way over in the Old Testament, which is called old for a reason; it's old! It is great to read back on history before Christ came, and through his Spirit we can receive revelation as we read the Old Testament through New Testament eyes. We are no longer in the old, we are now in the new, and it is time to embrace the new. You have a whole new inheritance, and it's his new Will and Testament for you. How can you receive all that you have by going back into the old? You can't. Once a new will comes in it makes the former will obsolete. The new Will is Christ risen and living in you. Jesus tells us in Luke 9:62, ***"No one, having put his hand to the plow, and looking back, is fit for the kingdom of God."*** We cannot begin and remain in Christ and then stop and go back into the old ways of religion, along with the traditions that people stipulated. It is Christ, and his Spirit alone that gives life, not man and his words. The only way forward is through his Spirit and living your life from out of him.

"God's ways and thoughts were higher than ours, until in the New Covenant he seated us in heavenly places next to himself in Christ Jesus."

Many different mixed religions have tried to kill the living Spirit within those who attempted to overshadow one another by trying to claim first place with God. The evangelical fundamentalists attempted to kill the Charismatic movement in the '70s. When a Charismatic move began to come and the Holy Spirit became very active and gifts were flowing, people were being baptized in the Holy Spirit. The people who came against it were the evangelical fundamentalists. Today we're moving with the Spirit of God, and the Spirit of Truth is taking us into grace, which is the finished work and authentic identity of the Fatherhood of God, and the sonship manifesting. Do you know who's trying to kill that? The Charismatics.

The most prominent people who oppose the message of inclusion, grace, and unconditional love are people in the Pentecostal-Charismatic movement. Once you begin sharing the truth and freedom in Christ, suddenly the friends you thought you had are now no longer your friends! They will be quick to tell you that you're in error and following heresy. They come at us with the traditions of men and well-established doctrines that have been accepted for generations.

They are forgetting they were the ones who were persecuted in the '60s and '70s by the fundamentalist evangelicals who refused to move to what the Spirit of God was doing then. Jesus also encountered this, and it is mind-blowing. Let's look at John 6:56 and see just how this works. Jesus was doing this revolutionary teaching, and in John 6:56, he said, ***"He who eats My flesh and drinks My blood abides in Me and I in him."*** Upon hearing this, everyone went *"Wow!"* Let me say to all those people who want to take the Bible literally, I don't know what you're going to do with that verse! If you take that literally, it sounds like cannibalism, and that's a hard teaching. The people who were with him, who were his disciples and a multitude of people, thought that this teaching was just too hard to take in! In John 6:60 we read, ***"This is a hard saying who can understand it?"*** They said that they could not receive it, and it was contrary to anything they had ever heard before. Jesus goes on to say in John 6:65-66 to say, ***"Therefore I have said to you that no one can come to Me unless it has been granted to him by My Father. From that time many of his disciples went back and they walked with him no more."***

Jesus lost many friends, including a bunch of his disciples. This wasn't the multitude, this wasn't the Pharisees or the Judaizers; these were his disciples. It says many of his disciples left and no longer walked with him because they couldn't go to the level that he was going, and this is what happens to many people today. We receive new revelation and live our lives from out of him, but as we keep moving forward there are many people, we have been friends with who will not want to go forward, preferring to stay where they are.

The friends you lose will be Charismatic, Evangelical, and religious people who cannot hear and understand the spiritual truths you are walking in; they will not relate to you. Some people do not have the revelation of his Truth, and others cannot be bothered to pursue the Spirit of Truth and look into those things you are saying, to hear for themselves. There are many reasons for this. However, the main thing is that you just keep walking with God and hearing him through a relationship for your life. Let us take some encouragement from Paul when he penned these words in Galatians 1:10. ***"For do I now persuade men, or God? Or do I seek to please men? For if I still pleased men, I would not be a bondservant of Christ."*** After a single teaching where they couldn't handle what Jesus said, he went from having a megachurch in John 6:59 to being left with just twelve people. In the natural that would not have been very encouraging, and this happens to us today when we receive a nice big bright light of revelation. We want to share our excitement with people on the grace we hear, yet some are not ready to receive it, and others just want to stay the same.

When we move from religion to revelation, we generally get a game-changing revelation that changes everything. There is no going back when you receive this lightning bolt of revelation. There is only one way, and that is forward. There is this defining moment that breaks you absolutely free. This revelation that comes in is like kryptonite to everything you've ever known; it just explodes all the false religious jargon you once believed.

We have the opportunity today to seek the grace and the joy of Christ that floods our hearts, even though we may have to walk through dark valleys and the loss of friends along with the things we've established. It is not people we are aiming to please; we are Christ's ambassadors, and we're administrating his love and freedom everywhere we go.

To end this chapter, I will leave you with some encouragement expressed by C. Baxter Kruger in his book; *"Jesus and the Undoing of Adam."* The love of the Father, Son, and Holy Spirit all in union together, passionately pursuing us in all of love's glory. The light is forever shining on all situations, and as you hear his voice within, choose the freedom that love, and grace offer you.

The Truth Again

~ "The life that God lives as Father, Son, and Spirit is not boring and sad and lonely. There is no emptiness in this circle, no depression or fear or angst. The Trinitarian life is a life of unchained fellowship and intimacy, fired by passionate, self-giving love and mutual delight. Such love, giving rise

to such togetherness and fellowship, overflows in unbounded joy, in infinite creativity and unimaginable goodness. The gospel begins here with this God and with this divine life, for there is no other. Before time dawned and space was called to be, before the heavens were stretched out and filled with a sea of stars, before the earth was summoned and filled with people and life and endless beauty, before there was anything, there was the Father, Son, and Spirit and the great dance of Trinitarian life. The amazing truth is that this Triune God, in staggering and lavish love, determined to open the circle and share the Trinitarian life with others. This is the one eternal and abiding reason for the existence of the universe and human life within it. There is no other God, no other will of God, no second plan, no hidden agenda for human beings. From the beginning, God is Father, Son, and Spirit, and from the beginning, this God has determined not to exist without us." ~

Chapter 8

~Fixed Position~

"Religion makes people act through heartless words of instructions for outward appearances. A person who hears by the Spirit within will naturally act from the rhythm of love, which needs no instruction."
Natasha Trezebiatowski

I started to move away from the mixture message and the things religion taught me around 2003, however, it wasn't until about 2008 that I had the revelation of the Fatherhood of God, which brought me down like kryptonite did for Superman! I had always prayed as we do to our Father and I listened to the name *"Our Father,"* but I never heard it with an understanding of what that word really meant, so it never became a part of me. When I finally had the revelation of the Fatherhood of God, it changed my whole view of God. I now saw him as a Father, and when I understood his love, the Father's love, it blew up my whole concept of eternal conscious torment. It instantly took away everything I had believed. I then began walking in grace, along with the liberty and freedom the love of the Father brings us, and I abandoned all the laws and standards I had been raised in and taught.

We all have our own story about how Christ led us into his grace and unconditional love of the Father. If you are just starting this journey, let me encourage you to keep going and press into God. Christ within you will reveal all the truth to you.

Now for Paul, his journey began on the road to Damascus where he had a full encounter with Christ and his love. However, prior to this Paul had to go through some things to get to the place where grace was revealed to him and remove all the religious bondage he had lived under. Paul's revelation in Galatians 1:15-16 became the centerpiece of his message that he delivered to the Gentiles, and it reads, ***"But when it pleased God, who separated me from my mother's womb and called me through his grace, to reveal his Son in me, that I might preach him among the Gentiles."*** Remember, although the Gentiles were pagan worshipers and knew about the Judaizes, they also believed they were separated from God and not included in his love.

The revelation Paul revealed is Christ *in* you, which radically changed how he saw himself. Paul now saw himself as always being the possessor. Even when he was persecuting the church and killing Christians, Christ was in him. How radical it must have been for Paul to have that revealed to him; that Christ has always been in him, even when he was doing very destructive and deadly things to people. If only he knew Christ before then, of course he would never have done the things that he did. I am sure many of us can relate to having feelings of remorse for something we did before we met the person of grace and unconditional love, Christ Jesus.

No person on this earth would ever harm and hurt another human if they had the revelation of his unconditional love within them. All our training from previous generations that taught us lies about God has made us hard-hearted and conditioned us for outward appearances, meanwhile our heart was churning on the inside with deadly ambitions. Paul didn't have the revelation or preach that Christ was revealed to him, it was far more intimate than that. He was telling everyone that Christ is *in* you Gentiles. He was saying to those who were pagan worshippers and had no spiritual background, nor any real idea who God was, that they had Christ *in* them! This was revolutionary to say the least! How powerful to be told that you have Christ in you, and not because you did anything or prayed the prayer, tithed, or did one of the numerous religious obligations. Paul said just as you are, Christ is also. The Greek word for *"In"* (meaning *in* Christ) is the word *"En"* it means *fixed position and in place.* Paul said that it pleased God to reveal the Christ that had a fixed place within me, and Christ is within *all* humans. That is the gospel of Jesus Christ, who is in you, the hope of glory.

"Life will change dramatically when you stop with the I am not, and be like your Father and just go with I am."

The religious barricade has been smashed down. We no longer have our blinders on. Christ within is revealed to us, and we can go anywhere in the world and tell people that Christ is in them. This eliminates any ideas that a person has to do something to receive Christ and allow him to come and live inside of them. It eliminates the idea of separation, and the idea of the haves and the have nots. It eradicates the idea that some people are in while others are out and destined for hell because they didn't do some things or say a few words. This totally removes the pressure to save all people for Jesus, because if you don't, then he will never live in them and they will go to hell. We witness and reveal Christ within people so they get a chance to know him, and just like you, they get to be released from prison and all kinds of fears, anxieties, and oppression the world puts on them. When you know the marvelous truth about God's unconditional love and all fear has left you, all you will want to do is let everyone know this incredible gift that God has for them. We then evangelize out of love, not from fear, as God says in 1 John 4:18, ***"Perfect love casts out all fear, because fear involves torment."*** I have heard testimonies of people who have been absolutely tormented out of fear they must evangelize and reach people for Christ every day, and until they do, they cannot rest. Torment is terrible and can grip us in all kinds of areas. In our lives, it is only through God's love that a person can be released from this prison.

Religion has manufactured the idea that we need to invite Jesus into our hearts and lives, yet that is not at all what Scripture tells us. Let us look at Colossians 1:26-27, ***"The mystery which has been hidden from ages and from generations, but now has been revealed to his saints, to them God willed to make known what are the riches of the glory of this mystery among the Gentiles; which is Christ in you,***

the hope of glory." Christ in you and me, and all of humanity is the mystery that has been revealed. This is a powerful awakening to what has already been done for us and is true.

The church mixes the whole idea up by taking what Jesus said to one man in the middle of the night in John 3:3, explaining to him that he must be born again from above. Jesus was talking to him about something that had yet to happen with his resurrection and ascension when we all received the Holy Spirit, that is people in the past, present, and future. Once we receive his Spirit within us, we are then born again from above and are all in union with him, and we are a brand-new creation. So, at the time Jesus was talking to Nicodemus, he was speaking about what was to come. Now, of course if Jesus had outlined how it was all going to take place, Nicodemus would not have understood or probably not have believed him. We are not making the old into something new and regenerating to start over again. We don't need to be cranked up! We have a wholly changed new creation's DNA within us. This was something the planet had never seen before until the day of Jesus Christ's ascension.

In 2 Peter 1:4, Paul says, ***"By which have been given to us exceedingly great and precious promises, that through these you may be partakers of the divine nature, having escaped the corruption that is in the world through lust."***

When Paul speaks here about the divine nature, he is not suggesting that you get just a little bit of it. There's no junior divine nature, and Jesus has a big senior divine nature. When you have the divine nature, you've got it all. His divine nature took up residence within you when you were co-resurrected with Jesus, and co-crucified, co-buried, co-ascended, thus creating a new creation within you. We may have read Galatians 1:16, that Christ is in us over the years as I certainly have for the last 50 years, but have we actually heard it? Do we see with our spiritual vision what Paul is saying, that all humans have within them the Christ Spirit? This huge revelation from Christ was revealed to him, and in him, and every person on the earth. One is given the connotation that Christ is still on the outside, and we are calling and praying to a God from the Old Testament. However, Paul is revealing through his Christ-given revelation that Christ is *in* him and all humans. Religion has taught us that we have been cut off and totally spiritually separated from him, and now we all need to take ahold of Christ's hand, and then he will take your hand in his, enabling you to be connected together! Religion always implies that you are separated and need to do something to receive God into your life. There is nothing you need to do and there are no introductions. We read in Colossians 1:26-27, that there was a mystery hidden from past generations, but now it has been revealed to everybody, including the pagans who worship some human made deity, that they all have Christ within them, the hope of glory. When Jesus walked the earth, he ate and socialized with all of society, including the drunks, the prostitutes, and even the tax collectors. These were all people that society and religious people would distance themselves from.

He was demonstrating God and showing God's love for all people. That was the living picture of what was to come, with his Spirit that would be in all people with no exclusions.

Those living and walking in a wrong manner are people who need to know that Christ is in them and that they can live a victorious life in him. The very reason evil and horrible things happen in this world is because they have not had the revelation of Christ within revealed to them. This is the message we need to tell them at the prisons, the halfway houses, and in every church across America and around the world. All people need to hear the message that Christ is in you. That was Paul's message and the divine nature/Jesus appeared to Paul on the Damascus road, and what he revealed to him was the Christ that was in him. The Christ that is in you is the result of the end of the first Adam and the placing of the last Adam in every man. When Jesus went to the cross, all humanity went to the cross with him. The old Adam died, and that race of man died, and there is no Adam anymore. I need to be a little bit legal with you and point it out in Scripture so you can read it for yourself. In Romans 5:19 it says, ***"For as by one man's disobedience many were made sinners."*** That was Adam, and as a result of his disobedience people copied him by going alone in this world through the mind separated from God. We all got into error and wrong thinking. Because we were duped, we didn't know our authentic identity, so we began to act in the same separated self-seeking manner as Adam. In Romans 5:19 Paul says, ***"So, also by one Man's obedience many will be made righteous."***

It is Christ's righteousness that took up a fixed position in you. Righteousness is a man; it is Jesus the Christ. It is the result of the last Adam, who is Christ, that took up residence in you. Because of his death, burial, and resurrection, you and Christ are one. When you have the revelation that Christ is living in you, what do you do then? What did Paul do? We find the answer in Galatians 1:15-16 (paraphrased) when he said, ***"I did not immediately confer with flesh and blood after I got this revelation of the Christ that was in me nor did I go up to Jerusalem before those who were Apostles before me but I went to Arabia, I went into the desert."***

Paul had to let it all settle in, he had to get a handle on this profound revelation, and he needed time alone by himself to do all this. Paul needed time to let the Spirit of Truth continue working within him and receive more understanding. Coming out of religion is not easy. We might receive the Truth and realize Christ is in us, but then we need time to really understand what this means, and to learn and hear from the Spirit. Paul needed time. He didn't rush out and tell everyone around him about this truth. He didn't run straightaway to the apostles or rush off into Jerusalem or talk to the Gentiles about it. Paul was still young in his understanding, and if he would have rushed out to the church and started sharing this tremendous revelation, they would have talked him out of it and called him a heretic, saying he fell into deception, which is exactly what we will hear when we go out and share the truth. Because people will try to discourage you, like Paul you will need time to be alone with God and work through some things that kept you trapped in a wrong belief and identity. So, once we receive the revelation, we need time to sit with God and remove all the religious bondage we still have hidden within us. Once you really see and the chains come off, then you are on fire with what God has shown you and you have his power within that nobody can shake from you.

When revelation comes, it's kind of a little fuzzy at first. You've got the idea and it's simmering in your spirit, but the more you let it cook the sharper it gets. I'm seeing some things I would love to share with you, but I'm not going to do it yet. I've learned my lesson from 15 years ago that revelation without foundation produces condemnation when shared. I've seen it in my own life. When I tell everybody everything that has been revealed to me without providing a foundation, their lives produce condemnation towards you and me. Paul didn't run up and begin to blab everything that he saw. He went out into Arabia before returning again to Damascus, and then after three years he went up to Jerusalem to see Peter. (Galatians 1:16)

Paul didn't want to tell every person, instead he needed to pick one guy to share his message with, so he went to James and he spent 15 days with him. In Galatians 1:18-23 (emphasis added) we read, ***"But I saw none of the other apostles except James the Lord's brother, now concerning the things which I wrote to you indeed before God I do not lie, afterward I went into the regions of Syria and Cilicia and I was unknown by faces to the church of Judea which were in Christ but they were hearing only he who formerly persecuted us now preaches the faith which he once tried to destroy and they glorified God in me."***

What is the message Paul is trying to get across to us? He's saying in Galatians 1:18-23 that when he went back home he stepped out a little bit, and then he began travelling around a little bit and sharing his testimony with people in the churches. He began sharing with believers what Christ had shown him and how Christ transformed his life through his Spirit within. Paul continues to say that he didn't really go out and make a big deal out of it and rent out an auditorium, nor did he put out flyers or advertising material to try and draw large crowds. Instead, he casually went about sharing his conversion in Christ with those who were around him.

He said in Galatians 1:24 that it really worked because they began glorifying the God they saw was in Paul, and they saw his total transformation into the likeness of Christ. When the release comes, you will go easy with it, and Christ will direct you to where to share your testimony of Christ within. Then people will notice his light within you and confirm it, and this will be fruit that is produced, just like they glorified the Christ that was in Paul.

There's this road that comes from religion to revelation, and Paul travelled it just like we have all done in varying forms. Let's read what Paul came out of in Galatians 1:13-14. ***"For you have heard of my former conduct in Judaism, how I persecuted the church of God beyond measure, and tried to destroy it. And I advanced in Judaism beyond many of my contemporaries in my own nation, being more exceedingly zealous for the traditions of my fathers."***

Paul was traveling along the road when the revelation hit him in Galatians 1:15 as we read, ***"But when it pleased God, who separated me from my mother's womb and called me through his grace."*** At precisely the right time God revealed to him the Christ that was within him. This is the point where

Paul's whole life changed, and here's the message that is for us today. When we encounter Jesus and the light comes on, there is going to be an internal upheaval and major changes to how you once saw God. All that self-righteousness, law-imposed behavior, and all the modifications you went through trying to make your actions line up, which all falls under what we call Christianity, will all drastically change.

The powerful thing about light is that it always dispels darkness. Darkness cannot stand in the presence of even the smallest amount of light. When you are filled with light and love it eliminates all fear of torment, and suddenly it's a very different world. The Christ that is in you will illuminate and come alive from within to the outer being, and he takes away all your trying and doing efforts that religion imposed on you. Suddenly, all your doing is like filthy rags. The Christ that is in you is going to open your eyes and change your thinking about some things, and as he does, his grace and unconditional love from within you will be like a fountain springing up in your life. The confidence that grace will produce in your life will reach out and give life-giving water to everyone around you.

As you move from religion to revelation, the first thing you will begin noticing is this amazing confidence which stemmed from out of his, beginning to rise up in you; and as you continue on in your relationship with the Christ in you, his love and grace will secure you. His grace within you will not try to affirm you by your outer works and behavior created through the laws of your church. You won't feel the need to do anything other than rejoice in him and allow him to shine through you, and from out of him you will naturally do what is right and beneficial. It is a natural loving response to a loving Father who loves you. We read in Ephesians 4:7, ***"But to each one of us grace was given according to the measure of Christ's gift."*** Grace is a gift from Christ. It is the very person of Christ and he has gifted himself in your spirit, you are both connected.

It's going to take us ages to come to get to the bottom of the grace he has demonstrated towards us in Christ Jesus. When we suddenly know that he brought us in by his grace, we can also understand that he is not expecting us to keep it by any of our own actions.

That is a phase you kind of go through as you come out of religion and into revelation. In Galatians 4:6-7 (paraphrased) Paul said, ***"There's one God the Father who is above all and through all and in all that God kept you and brought you in by grace."*** He'll keep you by grace as you see your loving Father taking full responsibility for you. He didn't ask you, he just graced you.

We have earthly fathers who are good. They provide for their children and we never really thank them for all the security and protection they provide for us. We might make some crazy mistakes, yet if a father is good, he will not abandon us. He is going to keep providing meals and a safe place for us. If our earthly fathers who are good provide everything for us and we never even said thank you, how much more is our heavenly Father going to provide for us. This is even more amazing to know you have the best Father, especially if you were not raised in a home with a good father.

You now know that you can come to your loving Father, who is going to look after you and provide for you. Everything you have been through and are going through, he is with you; and he will not leave you, ever.

I will finish this chapter with some Scriptures you can mediate on that the Father has promised you: God will never leave you (Deuteronomy 31:6), God will protect you (2 Thessalonians 3:3), God will give you strength for every battle (Isaiah 40:31), and God will never stop loving you (Ephesians 3:17-19).

~"I desire for you to become intimately acquainted with the love of Christ on the deepest possible level; far beyond the reach of a mere academic, intellectual grasp. Within the scope of this equation God finds the ultimate expression of their image and likeness in you. So that you may be filled with all the fullness of God! Awaken to the consciousness of their closeness! Separation is an illusion! Oneness was God's idea all along! Father, Son and Spirit desire to express themselves through your touch, your voice, your presence; they are so happy to dwell in you! There is no place in the universe where God would rather be!"
~ Ephesians 3:19 Mirror Bible

Chapter 9

~Bible Inerrancy~

"Saying that God will never reveal anything that is not in the Bible pretty well makes the Bible the fourth Godhead, and limits the voice of God...My advice is, don't get caught in that religious trap." Don Keathley

In this chapter we will look at the false teaching regarding the inerrancy of the Bible and how damaging this belief has been for countless people, who, over the years have endlessly tried to do things to please God because God said it's in the Bible. Once you come into the marvelous revelation of Christ within you, there will be an inner reassurance that comes from knowing him, along with an awareness that you possess all things. You no longer need to wait for the Holy Spirit to show up, and you don't have to go to all the mega-churches to find the presence of God, because you have the assurance and confidence that Christ is in you, and you indeed can have all things.

We read in Romans 8:32, ***"He who did not spare his own Son, but delivered him up for us all, how shall he not with him also freely give us all things?"*** You are now the possessor of all things, and to receive freely is to spend time with Christ and learn of him. Once you undo all the religious bondage, you will start seeing evidence of receiving what Christ has for you. It's a journey, a marathon, not a 100-yard dash, for there is no finish line. Christ is eternal, and you are eternal with him. It is a constant unveiling of greater revelation and truth that you will walk in as he shines the light on different aspects of your life.

When I grasped the revelation of grace and unconditional love and knew I already have everything, it changed my prayer life. I can't tell you the last time I asked God for something in prayer because I have already been freely given all things in Christ. If God so loved everyone in the world that he gave his only Son so that he could be in every human, then we are assured that God has also met every single need. Have you noticed that Jesus never prayed to have any of his needs met?

Jesus never prayed for finances. Why did he never pray for a place to live? Why did Jesus never pray for a donkey to ride? Why did Jesus never pray for any personal needs to be met? It makes you think. I have often heard it said, *"Well, that was Jesus, he was God, he could have anything."* You have Christ in you, 100 percent, and you are 100 percent human. So, you have everything that Christ has, the only difference is that you may take a little time to receive the revelation of all you have because you might need to undo some false thinking. It's learning how to unwrap the gift within you, but once it's fully opened it reveals everything inside.

Jesus lived from out of his Father's source and supply, and in John 16:15 we read, ***"All things that the Father has are Mine. Therefore, I said that he will take of Mine and declare it to you."*** This is what Paul means with his revelation of Christ in you. Christ brings everything when he takes up residence in you. Paul says in Galatians 2:20, ***"I have been crucified with Christ, it is no longer I who live, but Christ lives in me; and the life which I now live in the flesh I live by faith in the Son of God, who loved me and gave Himself for me."*** Paul lived his life out of Christ, whereas he once lived his life from out of himself through outward religious actions. Paul heard from God within, and he was directing and guiding his life, giving Paul all things that pertain to his life. When you come out of religion and into revelation, you will notice that you have a righteous consciousness. With Christ's revelation within you, all of a sudden, the sin consciousness goes away, replaced by the righteousness consciousness of Jesus, for the two cannot dwell in the same habitation.

"Who has saved us and called us with a holy calling, not according to our works, but according to his own purpose and grace which was given to us in Christ Jesus before time began." 2 Timothy 1:9

When the light comes in, the darkness must go; and when the righteous consciousness comes in, the consciousness of works has to leave. Grace himself displaces anything that seeks to create a sin consciousness. Effortless change comes as you recognize Christ within you, and when you release the Christ within as you see, you change. Not that you're trying to change; you do not have to put any effort into it because it will happen naturally from out of him. It would be best if you heard this by the Spirit, because listening by itself is very superficial. However, hearing is when it enters your spirit, and that word becomes your flesh.

Most of us came from backgrounds where we took the Bible as our absolute guide and unfailing source of all things; the religious mindset. We read the words and then try to do the right actions to please God outwardly. Once grace enters your mind and Christ in you is revealed, you will see a change and the Spirit is now first in your life, and when you are living from out of him, reading your Bible is secondary. Don't get me wrong, the Bible is a tremendous source of wisdom, and I do believe we should read it. The difference is, we don't look at it as a performance manual for trying to obtain the right performance for God. It is now a wonderful book that holds great revelation as Christ reveals it to you through your relationship with him. Then, from out of your relationship with him, you will conduct yourself according to him, which moves you away from yourself. The change in reason is that we now hear the Spirit of Truth as we read our Bible who bring revelation and understanding which naturally transforms us through our relationship with him, which is the tree of life. We don't read the Bible to find out what to do and what not to do, how to live and how not to live and then do our best to perform outwardly; that's the Tree of The Knowledge of Good and Evil. That is the cold, distant book that is dead, it's just words and there is nothing more to come out of it. The Bible will come alive as you read and study, seeing Jesus in your relationship with him.

There are about 40,000 religious denominations and mixture messages out there who have taken the Bible to make it a guidebook for life. That is not the guide to life. The Spirit of Truth that resides within you is the guide to your life. If you've lived the journey from religion to revelation, you might feel a little bit angry. I have dealt with a lot of people who are hostile towards the church and disappointed in everything the dead religion fed them. You will find people who react differently, and it never made me angry or mad at my Seminary professors. I was never angry over the years that I wish I could reclaim from while

I was in school because I don't teach any of it, and I don't believe most of it anymore. If you are feeling angry and hostile within, then I have some advice for you. There is no point in letting the past make you angry. It was the journey you were on at the time, and now you have a fresh understanding and new revelations to embrace as you move forward.

There are some valuable things you learned from out of it all, which may help someone trapped in religious bondage. In every negative situation, God will reveal a positive outcome that you can learn from. Go by what God is revealing to you today in the now, not yesterday. You want freshly baked bread, not stale, dry moldy bread; it is the healthy nutrients that stem growth. We need to move on, just as the apostle Paul did when he had the revelation knowledge of God's grace and unconditional love. He moved away from the clutches of religion and never looked back. In Philippians 3:13 he says, ***"Brethren, I do not count myself to have apprehended, but one thing that I do forgetting those things which are behind and reaching forward to those things which are ahead."*** You cannot go forward by looking behind. You must press on and learn more about Christ and then walk together in a relationship with each other.

There is no point in looking into things and saying, *"Well, I don't believe that, and it's not true,"* until finally, you don't believe anything anymore. When you deconstruct from religion, it is important to continue pressing into Christ and allowing him to continue teaching you. Some people move out of religion, but through their anger and hostility they fail to press into Christ. They have no faith in anything, no longer knowing what to believe. They are so angry with their former pastor and teachers. My advice is to let it go because there is nothing to gain by being angered by the past, but you can learn from it. I look back at the years that I taught a mixture message, but I didn't know it was a mixture message. I thought it was the truth, but it laid a good foundation for me to discern religion from revelation. So, perhaps look at that time you spent in religion as being something constructive, like Paul did. We don't read about Paul getting angry over what he used to believe in when he came to the revelation of Christ within. He just said, "That's who I used to be, and I got rid of it, and now it's gone, and this is who I am now." Let the Spirit of Truth lead you and submit to the Christ in you, based on everything you experience from this point forward.

In writing to Timothy, Paul said this in 2 Timothy 3:16, ***"All Scripture is given by inspiration of God and is profitable for doctrine, for reproof, for correction, for instruction in righteousness, that the man of God may be complete, thoroughly equipped for every good work."***

We have all read this Scripture and heard through our fundamental evangelical teachers that the Bible is totally inerrant because in verse 16 it says that all Scripture is given by God's inspiration and is profitable for doctrine and instruction. I want to point out something here and shed some light on this passage on what Paul meant when he said that God inspires all Scripture. I want to shed an entirely different perspective on this Scripture than what you have heard. In Young's Literal translation or in the Concordant Literal Translation, you will notice brackets around the word ***is,*** or sometimes it's in italics because in the original translation the word is not there. When we say all Scripture ***is***, this implies that everything in the Bible ***is*** inspired. When you remove the word ***is***, the verse takes on a totally different meaning.

When you take the ***is*** out of there, *all Scripture inspired by God* reads different than saying God inspires all Scripture. Do you see the difference? When we read the correct translation, *that all Scripture inspired by God,* this opens the door to the fact that maybe some of it is not inspired. This is an important consideration. Am I saying that all Scripture is not inspired? Well, let's talk about what inspired means. I want you to understand that when Paul wrote these letters we are studying, he had absolutely no clue that there would be a book called the Bible, consisting of 66 individual books composed of 39 in the Old Testament and 27 in the New Testament. Paul had no idea that what he wrote to all the churches would be included in the Bible, and he was not aware of there being a New Testament Bible at all!

He wrote to the Christians in Southern Turkey to address situations and problems specific to them at that time, and it's the same in Ephesus, Philippi and Colossae. He's writing to a group of believers and addressing situations and problems that were peculiar to them to encourage them and each region or city with different needs and facing various dilemmas. You have to keep in mind that these letters are for two different particular groups of people.

In Ephesians, Paul makes it clear that he's writing to the church at Ephesus, and in Philippians, Paul makes it obvious that he's writing to the Christians at Philippi, and in Colossians he writes to the church at Colossae. What he said to the church at Ephesus may or may not apply to the church at Philippi. And what he says at Philippi may or may not apply to the Christians at Colossae. It's like instructing children, you give one child instructions that may not be relevant to the other child. Let me give you a quick example. Let's say you have a child in school that's not very motivated. To this child you say, "You can do better. I want you to get your grades up, you need to spend more time studying. When you come home, I don't want you going outside to play until you get your homework done. I'm going to be looking closely at your grades, and you better get on the ball."

Now to the other child who is really excelling in school, and is diligent and disciplined in their studies, and gets all As, if what you said to the first child were to be taken by this child who is diligent, he may have a nervous breakdown. What you said to the first child is absolutely not appropriate to say to the second child. When we read Paul's writings, you need to come into the full realization of who he is speaking to and what problems each church was facing, and that the message he was trying to get across to each of them was sometimes different. This doesn't mean you can't learn from it, but you need to understand that it's not written to you. It's written for us but not directly to us. The Spirit of Truth is the inerrant guide, and the Spirit of Truth will take what he says in one letter and break it down for you. There have been times that I've read through Galatians, Ephesians, Philippians, and Colossians, and seen something entirely different. This is the Spirit of Truth bringing something that's not in black and white and suddenly making it true and relevant in my life for today, which is living in the now, this moment. Yesterday's revelation and teaching may have been a fit for me then because that's where I was at, but today I may be in a different mindset, and God will speak to me accordingly. We must remember he is the living word, and what he says will be different depending on what each day brings you. The Spirit of Truth is the inerrant guide.

The word *inspired* that we read in 2 Timothy 3:16-17 means; *God-breathed or contains the breath of God.* The Greek word for inspiration means that it is God-breathed. I think that's why people have decided that it's inerrant, because they assume it is all God-breathed. And because it has the breath of God on it, it is therefore inspired and inerrant. I want to remind you that everything God breathes on is not error-free. Did God breathe the breath of life into Adam? Was Adam error-free? I don't think so! Don't you and I contain the breath of God? You and I wouldn't be alive if we didn't have the breath of God in us, and we are not error-free. We inhale and exhale the breath of God, and it's our very essence of life. The truth is we are inerrant as humans, but we do make mistakes even though we know and trust in the One who is perfect and has completed everything for us; Christ Jesus. To say something is God-breathed and inerrant would be presumptuous. It would be a quantum leap that I am not sure the Father ever meant when Paul was writing to Timothy. I want to implant two specific beliefs into your spirit, which are two particular theories or beliefs on how God-breathed or who inspired Scripture. I want to acquaint you with two methods of inspiration, the first one is called the dictation or verbal inspiration theory. This theory says that the human role in writing Scripture was purely mechanical and that God, through the Holy Spirit, told the writers word for word what to write. That view takes the position that the Bible was like an executive memo, and God is dictating a letter to his administrative assistant, which was the Bible writer. The administrative assistant would take shorthand word for word, exactly what the executive, who is God, wanted to be penned in the letter and then sent out to somebody. The writer in the dictation theory is totally under the control of God. The writer was just an instrument. Fundamentalists and evangelicals hold to this dictation theory. The dictation theory people are the King James Bible only people. They hold fast to that version of the Bible as the correct copy and being error-free, while every other version of the Bible is mistaken.

They believe in a theological term called ***"Sola Scripture,"*** or the idea that only Scripture contains the authority for faith and practice. It is absolutely the crème de la crème, and there is absolutely no place for revelation outside of a literal interpretation of the King James Bible. The Bible addresses every problem perfectly, and this group of people use the Bible to prove the Bible, and they come back to you and say, *"Well, the Bible says."* The authority and practice that is allowed or viewed as the absolute truth is what the church's denomination says that it is, and that's why we have thousands of denominations today who claim what the Bible says is their foundation. The reason they hold to that Bible is that every other version diverts from the King James Bible. When you read the New International Version, the Good News, the Mirror, or whatever translation you like to read, you may see a little bit of a different slant than how the King James Version reads. They often use a verse such as what it says in Revelation chapter 22:19 (paraphrased), ***"If anybody adds to the Bible, adds to Scripture or takes away from Scripture they will be cursed,"*** and of course, the Scripture is the King James Version. They believe anytime you divert from the King James Version, there is a curse placed on you.

The King James version people will say that every other Bible translation is adding to it or taking from it, so, therefore, it's blasphemous. The Spirit of God, who is Christ within you, is the only truth that you need to hear.

We must all learn to resist the Judaizers who want to pull us back into rules and restrictions that limit the liberty you have in Christ. There is a lot of revelation and insight when we read different Bible versions and study the original Greek meanings.

"All of the things I grew up with that produced spiritual fear and anxiety like the second coming, rapture, seven year tribulation, eternal conscious torment, God's anger, inability to live perfection, sin, striving to be in God's presence, praying the right prayer with the right words, being sorry enough to be forgiven, were all dissolved with a revelation of pure, radical, hyper grace."

We need to resist our own mental inclinations to set up standards that we have to try to meet, or else God is not pleased. All those religious activities are not tied to the walk you have in the Christ who is in you. I want you to be free and enjoy your liberty, and I want you to know that you are being called to a life in full recognition on an ongoing unfolding basis of the Christ who is within you.

God has everything for you, and it has already finished. We bring into existence what is not seen through our faith and trust in Christ, who has finished everything for us. God has purposed everything you need for your life. There is nothing he is holding back from you because the Kingdom is within you. It is through your relationship with Christ that you have access to all things that God has for you, which you will know as you spend time with him. He will place in your spirit what he desires for you, which will become your desires, and you will have a vision that will manifest into your reality. All things are possible, although you won't need all things for your life. It may be possible for me to fly to Germany; however, it might not be a place I will ever visit because I have other places on my heart that I believe God has called me to travel to. I will step out by faith in the direction that he calls me, and through doing this I will only need the things God has for my life. Not everything will be of any benefit in our life, and hearing God for your life, you will discern what will be the correct way to go.

Here is a wonderful reading by Dan Stone and David Gregory from their book; *"The Rest of The Gospel."*

~ "God has already perfected those of us who are in Christ. We are complete in him (Colossians 2:10). We are his righteousness (2 Corinthians 5:21). We are holy and blameless and beyond reproach (Colossians 1:22). These truths are already our reality above the line, in the unseen and eternal realm, in God's kingdom, in our spirit. These are the eternal, unchanging truths of our identity as new creations, as sons and daughters whom God has birthed (John 3:3-6). Below the line, however, in the seen and temporal realm, we're in the process of being sanctified. We have needs. Our emotions fluctuate. Our behavior changes. We experience growth. The distinction between these two realms is vital to us for three reasons. First, in the here and now, God has designed his kingdom to work by faith. God could have placed the eternal in the visible realm. His eternal kingdom would then be plainly seen. But if he had done that, there wouldn't be any faith. Everything would be exactly as it appears to be, and faith would be pointless. But the whole universe operates on faith." ~

Chapter 10

~Dictation Theory~

"Our acceptance or rejection of Christ's loving sacrifice does not nullify its cosmic scope...No matter how much you reject Christ, he never fails to love and include you...You are free to reject him - but your rejection does not nullify his inclusion...You cannot dictate his character that way. You cannot make him cease being Love."
Cecil Cockerham

We will continue to explore the dictation theory of the Bible and some of the religious conditioning you may be accustomed to, which will help identify why it can still have a strong spiritual hold. Religion is a constant strain, and it's really a demonstration of unbelief. Rather than living inward through a continued relationship built on what He has already done, people attempt in their own strength to outwardly follow rules and regulations. There is nothing heartfelt in reading Biblical words and trying in your own effort to accomplish what Christ has done for all humanity. We are righteous in him, and as we join together in one union through our relationship, and our hearts naturally change to his mind and his ways of doing everything. We can enter any number of denominations today who all have a different take on what the Scriptures say. In the Catholic Church, there are many people who, even to this day, cannot read the Bible. Instead they believe what the priest tells them. If you are a Baptist, you believe what the Baptist tells you, and if you are Presbyterian, you believe in predestination, according to what the pastor or priest is telling you. If you are Charismatic, you believe what the Bible says clearly about the gifts, yet the Baptist says the gifts have passed away. You say, *"No, I believe what the Bible clearly says, that we all have the gifts till we come to the measure and the stature of the fullness of Christ."* They believe that we are not mature, and we're not in the unity of the faith, so what the prophets and pastors teach us about the gifts are not valid for today.

The dictation theory is very strict with the letter of interpretation. It is what the authorities, the church leaders, say it is according to their interpretation, and we need to understand that this approach is a dictation theory. It is the fundamentalists and evangelicals who hold to the dictation theory that God gave the Scriptures word for word to the writers. I teach you from my experience that there are so many variations to what the Scriptures say, but there is only one Spirit we hear from and are taught. I will add that there is another theory, which is *"Plenary"* inspiration, and this is the idea that God, through the Holy Spirit, gave the thoughts or the ideas and then guided or inspired the writer as he wrote his thoughts. The Father and the Holy Spirit inspired areas or topics or thoughts, but then the writer had the liberty to express what he said under guidance from the Holy Spirit. This leaves room for the personalities of the different writers and their writing style, which you can see vary distinctively between all the authors of the Bible. If we are in a dictation, then the Bible writers would all sound the same with identical types of personalities. However, that is not at all how the Bible reads. We can clearly see that all kinds of different characters were inspired by God and wrote out their encounters and what they heard from God. Plenary inspiration will leave room for you to see beyond what the writer is saying. Once you see the thought, then the Spirit of Truth can begin inspiring you to further see what the writer wrote.

The dictation theory is religious bondage. It leaves just the black and white or the red and white without regard to any other thought as to what the Bible has to say. The dictation theory will even take words like *"Hell"* that never appear in the original languages and words like *"Saved"* and totally redefine it to mean it's your ticket to heaven, or if you're not saved, then you're going to *"Hell."* That's not what saved means. Saved means; *wholeness, fullness, completeness*. The authorities have defined the word *saved,* and when you read that in your Bible or the word hell, you believe them. The dictation theory leaves no room for any variance or for you to do your own research into the original words and meanings because what they dictated to you is absolute. Religion has totally done its job programming people to follow their cold hard outer works and rules, leaving you with no room to be free to hear from God yourself through the Christ Spirit that is in you. They do a magnificent job of keeping you on the outside of God and holding you right where they want you, in their control.

"There is nothing to be accepted or rejected in the New Covenant. It's too late you have already been included. Now open your eyes to who you have always been and what you have always possessed. I dare you to try and get yourself unsaved."

In plenary inspiration, you can meditate and allow the Spirit of Truth to unveil or take you to a place beyond the black and white or the red and white. The word can go deeper than face value, which now allows you to explore the depths of a God beyond the words on paper. The words in themselves don't have life, which is why the dictation theory will never work. Only by the Spirit can we receive and know the truth and then walk that truth out.

People who adhere to the dictation theory have obeyed the Bible God, the fourth member of the Godhead, and they believe God dictated every word. Therefore, they reason that this is God himself that said every word. But the plenary inspiration adherents understand that the topics, the thoughts, and the ideas come to the writers from God, and then the writer began exercising some freedom in the expression of those thoughts, ideas, and topics under the direction of the Holy Spirit. God has made all of us unique and individuals. If he wanted robots that followed the same suit and order, he could have easily done this. However, God allows us the freedom to express what he impresses on our hearts, whereby everything we do and say will all be a representation of his truth, which will be rooted in love. This is the reason I can read a Scripture different from you. Because what the Spirit is saying for me in my life, the truth will be highlighted, yet for your life it may be a different revelation. However, God is truth, so everything we read in Scripture is all pure unconditional love and grace, which we interpret through his eyes of love. He is the inherent word of truth and that will never change. As we see his light, we share his light because there will be people who are facing similar situations that you have been through who need encouragement in Christ. This is why many people are attracted to certain ministers, because they can resonate with their message. It has touched their heart and there is familiar ground, along with excellent teaching founded on his love. The Bible was not meant to be taken word for word, it was always an inspired word for you to read but then allow God to shine his light and illuminate his word that is relevant for you, not somebody else.

I pastored for thirty-five years, teaching a mixed message of Old Testament laws and New Testament grace. Were there times that I knew I was speaking under an unction that was not me? Absolutely. Does that mean what I was saying was error-free? Absolutely not.

I might also look back five years from now and say I understand more now, and therefore I can add to what I am teaching you in this book. As the Holy Spirit opens our eyes to deeper dimensions, the revelations become stronger, and the picture becomes sharper and clearer. We have to allow for adjustments as we walk with God in our journey. We read how the apostle Paul transformed in each of his writings as he grew more and more with God each day. We depend on the Spirit of Truth within us to reveal the correct way in which to follow God, and we are going to make some errors along the way. We have a lot of our own false thinking and ideas that perhaps need to be adjusted. However, we are quick to change our minds when we see something that we never saw before.

With the dictation theory, you're not allowed that liberty. The fundamentalists get a doctrine set in concrete and there is no variation from it. There is no increasing it, and there is no clarification because what is written is set in stone. We go to church every Sunday, and we hear the same message and the same truth. It's just presented time and time again with repetition, so we can become grounded in it to where we don't question it. I hope that this has helped you see the different forms of religious bondage that we can be entangled in. I think it is important to be aware so that we can all be removed from the clutches of religion.

"Till we all come to the unity of the faith and of the knowledge of the Son of God, to a perfect man, to the measure of the stature of the fullness of Christ." Ephesians 4:13

We are on a journey to the freedom of sonship, and the call of the day is manifesting as sons and daughters of God who are fully matured and coming to a measure of the fullness and stature of Christ, through the unity of faith. To get there, we have to see exactly what he is trying to teach us from his Word, and that is where you will need your own individual freedom, not just to read the words and then try to obey, but listen to the Spirit within you. We read in Galatians 4:8, ***"But then indeed, when you did not know God you served those which by nature are not gods."*** Paul was conveying to the Galatian church that when we didn't know God, we had not yet received the revelation of who he really is, how he really is, and what his character and nature is like, so we relied on the people who made themselves gods of this world. We trusted in hearing what the pastor or priest was reading and saying without questioning any of it, nor did we look into it with God. Until the Spirit of Truth reveals his unconditional love and grace, we find ourselves running to people with their preconceived ideas and notions rather than listening to the Spirit within. The faster we can get rid of all preconceived notions and ideas and cut those cords and bonds off us, the more clearly we can see. The best way to do this is to ask God questions. If you want to know the truth of something go straight to the source. God will answer you, it might not be straight away because sometimes we are not ready to hear what God has to say. He will always answer you in the form of revelation, and it can happen through all kinds of ways, not just the Bible.

We have all served a god that we created in our mind, and we served a god through what we were told at church or somebody else imparted to us that was really not God at all. The Spirit of Truth today is breaking the Father out of the box of tradition we've put him in, and we are beginning to look at Jesus as being the full representation of the Father. We are now starting to rise up as sons and daughters of God and learning to tune into his Spirit and hear for ourselves, for our individual lives, through a relationship, not a book, as God always intended.

The Old Testament was not an accurate presentation and representation of the Father, so Jesus came to clear up all that mess. We have the prophets, Elijah, Jeremiah, Ezekiel, and others who could never say, *"If you have seen me, you have seen the Father."* Jesus was the one who came down from heaven to present and show us the Father and demonstrate heaven on earth. This is why he said in John 14:9 (paraphrased), ***"If you have seen Me, you have seen the Father."*** The Spirit of Truth today is taking God out of the box religion had put him into, and he's unveiling him for who he really is, and has always been.

Paul says in Galatians 4:8 that when we did not know God, before he had not been revealed, we served those by nature who were not God, and taught us through human-made religious methods. However, you can now see clearly because you have the Spirit of Truth residing in you. We are the sons and daughters of God right now as we read in 1 John 3:2, ***"Beloved, now are we are children of God."*** It has not yet been revealed to you, and you haven't seen everything the Father has for you. John said we would know when he appears once he's revealed, and it doesn't mean Jesus' second coming. What he means is, when we get a revelation of him. The emphasis John is making is that we will be like Christ because we have seen him, he has been revealed to us, and the more we are shown, the more like him we become.

However, religion's eyes made all humans separate from God since Adam made that first initial false perception. Adam created a god he thought was angry, judgmental, punitive, and totally separated from us. This caused him to run and hide, but the whole time God was calling Adam to come to him. The Father never acted in anger towards Adam or was mean and judgmental. He was protective of Adam. God moved him out of the garden and away from the tree of life, lest Adam eat from that tree and live in a condition far below the Father's plan for him for all eternity. God protected him, and the Father was never separated from Adam. God found Adam; he went and escorted him, and then drove him from the garden.

I was taught the god of Adam's perception, who was a misconceived, ill-conceived god he created in his mind, and this religion has been passed down from generation to generation until today. Thousands and thousands of years later, this god has become the false perception that has been ingrained in our minds. When someone comes along and begins to teach the Father, who is the representation of Jesus, and the Father that looks like Jesus, we say that is false. We believe a lie when the truth sounds better. Why is that? Because we have heard it repeatedly, that repetition has built up a stronghold within us to the point it can block our personal relationship with Christ. The god that Adam created in his fallen state of mind, who then passed it down through subsequent generations does not exist.

The fact remains that he's closer than our next breath. Here's what Jesus said in John 14:20, and this is the crux of the gospel. ***"At that day, you will know that I am in My Father, and you are in Me, and I am in you."***

The Father and the Son and all humans are intertwined. We are in a union together as one. God is one with everybody, however, not everyone believes in their mind that God exists, or perhaps they believe in the god of Adam. It is a matter of believing, as Jesus said in John 6:29, ***"This is the work of God, that you believe in Him whom He sent."*** When we have a relationship with God, we believe in him and trust him as we hear him in our spirit when he speaks to us. When you didn't know God, you were serving these things that by nature were not gods. You were off into paganism, worshipping trees, wind, sky, and even the stars! In Galatians 4:9, we read, ***"But now after you have known God, or rather are known by God, how is it that you turn again to the weak and beggarly elements, to which you desire again to be in bondage?"***

Paul is saying that we have embarked on this two-way discovery. First of all, we have come to know and understand who God is, and that he is the Father of all. As we read in Ephesians 4:4-6, ***"There is one body and one Spirit, just as you were called in one hope of your calling, one Lord, one faith, one baptism, one God and Father of all, who is above all, and through all, and in all, and in you all."*** We have one Father of all, and regardless of whether we recognize him as that or not, that's who he is. It is much to your advantage to recognize who he is and live in who he is, but there are thousands of people today who sadly are sitting in churches and have no idea that he is the Father of all humanity.

Religion has hoodwinked so many people into believing that he is only the Father of those who believe the way their church denomination has taught them. Maybe they said the magic prayer and confessed a few words from the Bible, or perhaps they were dipped in water. Maybe it is through speaking in tongues and all these other religious methods that have led countless people to believe that he only reveals himself to those special few.

Paul said to the Galatians that God reveals himself as the Father of all, and he's above all and is through all, and in all, so that's a one-way discovery. Paul reminds the Galatians of their revelation that they are known by God in a way that he has always seen them. ***"But now after you have known God or rather are known by God how is it that you turn again." (Galatians 4:9)***

That is a dynamic revelation, knowing you like he's always known you, and seeing you like he's always seen you. Then you begin to say that he is nothing like the god Adam planted in our mind or the god Moses revealed. This two-way discovery of knowing him and how he sees us opens the door to a tremendous revelation. Paul explains how people can come into God's unconditional love and then move right into human-made religious doctrines. In Galatians 4:10-11 (paraphrased), we read, ***"You observe days and months and seasons and years, you've gone back, and you've adopted man-made standards you Galatians."*** When you adopted a human-made standard, you have, of necessity, embraced a human-made God who demands that you keep the human-made standards.

Religion will keep you mentally busy so that you will keep up the false god's expectations of performance and make sure that you satisfy him. The only god you are really satisfied with is the human god and his false godly standards he is imposing on you.

God was never looking to rule by laws, and he did not create people to be slaves. Humans have done that to humans, but it was never God's plan. In fact, God never wanted animal sacrifice. God never desired blood sacrifice. We read this in Psalm 51:16. Let's read what David said, ***"For you do not desire sacrifice or else I would give it, you do not delight in burnt offerings."*** God never wanted that kind of offering, it was people that wanted the laws and the children of Israel at the foot of Mt. Sinai. God wanted all humans to come up to know him and to have fellowship with him, but the people said no. They told Moses they were afraid of God, and they didn't want to go up there. They insisted that Moses go up there on their behalf and find out what God wanted them to do, and they wanted Moses to come back down and tell them, and then they would be happy to do what God asked.

That's how the birth of the law came, and animal sacrifice. It was man who needed a way to cleanse his own conscience and make himself/herself feel like they were in a right position with God. He never needed anybody to kill a bull, a lamb, or a dove, or anything in the way of an animal sacrifice. That was an institution that man created, but God went along with it because it made people feel good. Jesus said in Matthew 22:40, that all of this hangs on two things, all the law and all the prophets. However, Jesus puts everything so simple and easy, so that nothing is complicated or hard. He said in Luke 10:27, all you need to develop is loving God with all your heart, all your soul, all your mind, and all your strength. And when you do that, there is something that will naturally happen; *you will love your neighbor as yourself.*

You can't help but love your neighbor as yourself with unselfish love and a giving love once you develop the love you have for the Father, and you have the revelation of his love for you. The Father's love now envelops you, and out of this enveloping comes a natural flow of loving your neighbor as yourself. It takes all the law and all the prophets out of it. We move out of religion with all of its human-made laws and rules and into a relationship with God, our Father through Christ Spirit, who lives in us.

As David Adams said in one of his article posts, everyone has inherited the earth, and we live here on it with Christ as joint heirs, we walk everything out as we hear from our Father.

~ "Most people have very little idea of what Jesus did when he died upon the cross. If you listen to what is preached in most churches, you will come away thinking that all Jesus did was make a way for you to possibly get to heaven someday after you die. This is nowhere near the truth. Don't get me wrong. I still believe that our spirit goes to be with the Lord when we die. Jesus came to accomplish much more than that. He came to make us free from the law of sin and death. He came to make mankind free from the dominion of sin. If you listen to most preachers, they will tell you that you're just a sinner saved by grace. In reality, you are a saint that might still sin sometimes. The trouble is most preachers are preaching that we are under the law instead of under grace. At best, they are preaching a mixture of the two. Paul called that another gospel. We cannot live under law and Grace at the same time. You're probably asking yourself that since we are under grace can we do anything we want to. God forbid. If you understand Grace correctly, then you will know that Grace teaches us to live godly in this world.

Almost everywhere that missionaries have gone to spread the gospel, they have usually spread a mixture of Law and Grace. These two are in conflict with one another and cannot be reconciled. It keeps people trying to earn what has already been freely given.

The true gospel says that God has reconciled the world to himself. The true gospel says God keeps no record of wrongs and remembers our sins no more. We have a totally new slate, and God isn't writing our sins upon it. He has written upon it that we have been made the righteousness of God in Christ.

If we only believed these things that Jesus did, our lives would be totally different. We wouldn't be trying to escape this world. We would be receiving it as an inheritance. We would know that we are joint heirs with Jesus Christ and that we have inherited the earth. We would know that God remembers our sin no more, and neither would we. Our conscience would be cleansed from sin, and we would walk in Eternal Life, experiencing intimacy with the Father and the Son through the Holy Spirit.

Our Royal Daddy, thank you for being so patient with us as we grow into maturity in order to reveal your kingdom here on earth. May every blind eye be open, and every deaf ear hears the clear Proclamation of the kingdom of God. May we learn to walk in the Glorious Liberty of the sons of God."~

Grace and peace. Amen.

David Adams

Chapter 11

~Covenant or Contract~

"It is written on our hearts… we are the New Covenant living epistles."
Lisa Wentworth Couture

It is important that people know the difference between a covenant and a contract. The mixed message and religious institutions will hold you in bondage by using the wide variety of contracts they offer you. They are in a document form where you read their laws and then sign at the bottom, along with verbal agreements that state so long as you stick to their rules you are in, and you will be sure to receive the blessings of God. However, if you break those rules and do not stick to your end of the contract, the deal is off, and you are out. We hear this happening time and time again in the news, where a pastor is caught engaging in some misconduct and has been removed from the church. They did not comply with what the contract stipulated, just like a business deal, and so out they must go to keep the reputation of the "Business" going. That is not the heart of our loving Father, to establish a contract business system within the church. There are churches today that teach similar rules like; you can't go to movies, you can't dance, don't smoke, and definitely no drinking! They convinced themselves that they need to do more for God. They had gone back in their mind to the bondage they came out of and wanted to bring a few chains back in, as Paul said in Galatians 4:17-20 (paraphrased). ***"Religion zealously caught you, but not for good, they want to exclude you, they want to separate you, that you might become zealous that you might become entrenched in their doctrines. It's good to be zealous in a good thing and not only when I am present with you. My little children of whom I labor in birth again until Christ is formed in you, I would like to be present with you now and to change my tone, for I have a lot of doubts about you, I know you're going through some real trouble."***

Religion always tries to alienate you from knowing the truth and the gospel's simplicity, which is grace plus nothing. Religious doctrines don't want you hearing about grace. They want you to get sold out on Jesus plus whatever it is they're peddling. Many of us have had our pastor tell us not to read that book, and we better not attend that conference, and hear the speaker because he's from the devil and in error. Who are the people in error? Who are the people teaching heresy? Anyone who is adding to Jesus. All the laws, rules, human-made restrictions, and requirements that you cannot possibly keep. Error is living your life through human-made rules, void of a personal relationship with Christ. If you hear rules and laws being pushed in your church, then yes, they are in error and it is heresy, which is a mixture of teachings that blend religious laws with a little bit of Jesus' grace on the top. Jesus didn't come to abolish the laws. They are all good, and he fulfilled them all, but how we keep them is done through him, from out of our personal relationship with him. He will speak to you, and you will always want to do what is right and beneficial. The Galatian people experienced God's grace and unconditional love, yet over time they started blending in the Old Testament laws and conditions. We see the same thing happening within churches all around the world today. We have the incredible revelation of God's love and come alive, but then, over time something happens, and we start listening to human-made doctrines and the conditions they stipulate on us. Then slowly over time, as we hear them and receive our renewal contracts, we start to separate ourselves from the unconditional love of God. Paul experienced this with the Galatians who had moved backward and given up their freedom. He was seen as an enemy to the doctrine they created when they were combining the two together.

"Have I therefore become your enemy because I tell you the truth?" Galatians 4:16

Religion had snuck back in, and people were saying that Paul was not telling them the whole story, and they needed to add more to what Paul revealed. They suggested keeping certain rules such as circumcision and being watchful over the way you live so that you are holy before God.

What is religion trying to do? It tries to move you in all its human made forms to separate you further from the truth. Religious doctrines keep you under their control like an infant, so you don't grow; all you do is remain dependent on what they say. The religious teachers are very smooth in their approach, having a public speaking influence, and charisma that draws people to them through their fancy words to get people outside of grace; hooking them back into bondage. Sometimes you need to let go of friends you had back in your religious days because they will try to pull you back again. The best thing you can do is love them while remaining at a distance and, as you have the opportunity, minister the love and grace of God to them. Often, just like Paul, we look like an enemy because we are sharing the truth of God's unconditional love. Paul got really heated with them to make his point that they had gone back to religious garbage, and now they want to distance themselves from him when he was the one who brought them the truth! You will often notice this happening in your own life.

Many people will break fellowship and walk away from you because you no longer believe the same way they do. It happens time and time again. We all soon find out that we weren't really friends because religion builds fellowship around the same beliefs and doctrines. They are not interested in you as a person; it's all about doctrines. If it were about God's love, grace, and mercy, then you would not get attacked for following the unconditional love of God. They would still be your friend today because they care. There will be no unity of the faith so long as we group up by what we believe, and we're not willing to understand and accept somebody who believes a little different from what we believe. Don't let it become an offense when friends break from you. I know it stings, I know it hurts, and the best you can do is understand they are where you have been. You become the reflection of what you believe. You become the reflection of the love and grace you believe in, and the kryptonite to religion is grace. Religion will not want to be around pure grace by definition; they are diametrically opposed to one another.

This cult-type behavior happens all the time, and what Paul is talking about in this passage of Scripture, is they separated even from their own families when the family no longer believes the same. This separation, Paul said, is to bring you back into bondage and indoctrinate you. They will use verses and twist Scriptures to try and show you they are right, and they turn the verses to be about you. Paul, being aware of this, shares his concerns in 2 Thessalonians 2:1-3 (paraphrased). ***"Now brethren***

concerning the coming of our Lord Jesus Christ and our gathering together to him, we ask you, not to be soon shaken in mind or troubled, either by spirit or by word or by letter, as if from us, as though the day of Christ had come. Let no one deceive you by any means; for that day will not come unless the falling away comes first."

You and I have been raised in the Western Church, and it was an *"If-then"* gospel. You had to ***do,*** and then God will ***do*** and what we have is more of a contract than a covenant. A contract means; *an agreement for specific requirements that are made between two parties.* If I need a new roof on my house and contract with a roofing contractor, the contract will say if he tears the old roof off and makes all the repairs, and then put the new roof on and if it doesn't leak, then I will write him a cheque for the full amount of the contract agreement. However, if you don't do your part and put a faulty roof on, and I don't pay you the cheque the contract calls for, then we are not in agreement. A contract is, you do your part and I will do my part of the agreed deal. A covenant is different. It is two people entering into a relationship, and the strength of the stronger becomes that of the weaker.

Even if one person does not keep up their end of the covenant, the other party is still committed to it as long as they live. Doesn't this sound a lot like what marriage is supposed to be! Sadly, most people today take marriage as a contract. If you don't do what you agreed with me and you mess up, then I'm divorcing you and the contract is final. The marriage covenant is in it for the whole ride, the good, the bad, and even the very messy situations at times. I understand that people divorce due to traumatic circumstances, so please take heart; I am only sharing the difference between a contract and a covenant. God knows what you are going through within your covenant marriage and it is between the unity of all people involved to discern the best outcome founded through his love. The marriage covenant that God has with us, however, is different than how we are in this world. He does not break his covenant with us at any time, no matter what we have done nor how much we have separated ourselves in our mind from him. His relentless love is never ending. Through everything in life you can be assured of his one promise, that is he is always with you and he has never left your nor forsaken you, no matter what you have been through, are going through, or will ever go through. His love never fails, and it never ends.

Paul demonstrated this when he told Timothy, even if we are faithless, he remains faithful. That is a covenant. His faithfulness has nothing to do with our faithfulness; these are two separate issues. If it were a contract he would say, *"I will be faithful to you if you are faithful to Me."* Paul says it's a covenant, so even if we are faithless and don't hold up our end, and don't meet the stipulations, the covenant says that the other covenant partner is fully obligated to carry it through, even to their own hurt.

Now that's not what we learned in church. What we learned in church is the contract involves you praying the prayer, you do what you need to do to be obedient, disciplined, and then God blesses you. If you tithe, then the windows of heaven are open; however, if you don't tithe the windows are not open to you, and sorry, no blessings from God. That's a contract. This contract looks on Jesus as having a done deal; he has done his part, but his part is totally ineffective if we don't do our part. That's not a covenant that's a contract. We are not under a new contract; we are under a new covenant. The reason I preach at the Digital Cathedral online every Sunday is for one main reason. I do not want to be a part of a brick and mortar building anymore because it is contract-focused, and I want to talk covenant with people. I am not opposed to ministering in a building, and I may do that again one day, but it will be under the covenant of God.

Religion points at you and me and says, *"That's the falling away right there! Look at that. They've fallen away from the rapture, they're fallen away from believing in a literal eternal conscious torment, they have fallen away from the faith."* Religious people will say that grace/unconditional love, followers of Christ have fallen away from believing that the Bible is totally inerrant. To religious people that's the only guide there is in the truth, so they believe we have fallen away from it, when in reality they are the ones who have fallen away from the pure gospel of Paul. We don't need to throw that in their face, we just love them and demonstrate Christ.

Unless the falling away comes first and the man of sin is revealed, the son of perdition opposes and exalts himself above everything called God, which was religion then and religion now. We are zealous for grace and to represent grace, Christ, but religious people are zealous for themselves, and what the human-made rules are representing is very impersonal and cold.

Here is a tell-tale sign that grace has set you free. When you can be the same person no matter who you're with, and you can accept other people right where they are. You have no problem accepting them, but religious people will have a problem accepting you. Grace operates through love, while religion operates through their rules, and if you don't abide by their rules, then out you go.

If you join the Baptist church then you're like the Baptists; whichever denomination you pick, you become like them. Grace frees you from looking at churches and people, along with their rules and guidelines. Grace will take you within and as you are in this world, so too is Christ. We fellowship with each other to discuss Christ, encourage one another, and support each other through trying times. It is Christ whom we follow, and we don't necessarily need anyone because we are secure with knowing Christ within.

"It will seem to me if I need a Scripture to confirm what the Father speaks to me then one of the two are unnecessary."

Paul said he would travail for the people because he saw them going back and forth, from grace to religion and grace to law. Paul said that he would enter in until Christ is revealed in them, till he is fully formed in you, and he asked if the fullness of Christ was already in them. Absolutely he was. Christ's fullness already indwelt them, and the Spirit of Truth was in them, but what Paul was saying to them was he wanted Christ that is in them to be fully unveiled. Paul was working with them and laboring so Christ could be fully formed in them. He was continually teaching them so there would be no more going back and forth. They had not yet arrived at that place in their journey and in their walk as sons and daughters of God in their development.

In Colossians 2:9-10, it says that in Jesus dwells the fullness of the Godhead bodily, and you're complete in Him in whom the fullness of the Godhead dwells. The fullness of the Godhead dwells within you, and the way to know its expression is when you can be the same every day of the week with whatever group of people you are with, and you just let him begin to come forth out of you. Christ in you is the same yesterday, today, and tomorrow. He does not shift or move depending on people and what they do to you. It is we who move and can get caught up in what people do to us. Our response needs to come from Christ in all situations, not just in good situations. It is easy to be full of grace and unconditional love while things are going great, but how about when things are not so great? How about when people come at you and say and do all kinds of things that hurt you? How do you respond? As the saying goes, squeeze a lemon and you get lemon juice. What is on the inside will come out, and you won't get orange juice! If grace and unconditional love are dominating your life, then when you get squeezed that is what will come out. And if it doesn't, that's okay too. Accept where you are at and keep walking with Christ. He will get you to that place where he is revealed through all situations. It is not saying that we don't feel the hurt and the pain of horrible and hurtful situations, we do. How we respond in these situations will reveal how much we know Christ or how much we know of the world and its attitudes. There is always a right way and a wrong way to respond to all situations, and knowing Christ is going to set your heart straight.

We can pray for people just like Paul did when he said in Ephesians 1:18, ***"The eyes of your understanding being enlightened, that you may know what is the hope of his calling, what are the riches of the glory of his inheritance in the saints."*** The eyes that open are progressive, and this happens a little at a time. Do you remember back when you first had grace revealed? Your eyes opened just a little bit, and that made you hunger for more, and so your eyes opened further. Now you can't wait to get the next unveiling and get the next piece of the puzzle. You're hungry for more, and that's a good sign. Growing people should be hungry for more and more of this, and long to be more like him. There is a progression to this, and in Romans 8:14-18, Paul talks about being led by the Spirit. We should be led more by the Spirit today more than we were yesterday; it is a continual daily walk and growth. In Romans 8:17-18, Paul talks about the fellowship of his sufferings, that we might manifest the glory. Going through this process will mature us as it did Paul, who could finally say, as he came through the maturing process, that his grace is sufficient. Paul could say that his grace is sufficient, and his strength is made perfect through his weakness because he learned to draw his strength through Christ and see him through all the trying times he faced.

Paul wrote to the Galatians to get them consistent in their faith. What was creating the consistency or patience in their faith was the circumstances of religion pushing back against them. Patience is consistency under pressure, and you will never know patience until pressure pushes back. That's what the book of Galatians is about. Finally, you will say to God you have won the race, and you kept the faith because Christ in you taught you to stand and rest in every challenge. You will indeed say that God is good all the time.

We will end this chapter with a beautiful devotion for you to meditate on taken from Paul Gray's book *"Notes From Papa."*

~ *"To My wonderful child who knows Me, the only true God, I'm so pleased that you now know Me and have rejected the false god of religious imagination! You have been taught that God is against you, can't stand to be with you, and is terribly displeased with you because of your sin. I'm so glad you have rejected that "god" and embraced Me and know that I am good, I love you unconditionally, and I am totally for you! You have been taught that god has separated you from it, is distant, aloof, and watching you like a hawk while it keeps a meticulous record of every single mistake you have made and bad thoughts you've ever had. I'm so glad you have rejected that "god" and embraced Me ... who is in you and in whom you live and move and have your very being. You have been taught that god demands that you sacrifice, give, work and do-do-do to please it and that whatever you do will never be enough. I'm so glad that you have rejected that false "god" and that you know that you are My beloved child in whom I am well pleased and happy with! Jesus did everything for you in his finished work at the cross, and there is literally nothing for you to ever do to gain or maintain the right relationship I have included you in with Me! You have been taught that god's love is very conditional and that it stops the minute you take your last human breath unless you have said the right words in the prescribed way with the right attitude of the heart. I'm so glad that you have rejected that false "god" and accepted the acceptance that We gave you because of Our unconditional love which you can never be separated from! Not even death can separate you from Our love! You have been taught that you should fear the angry god and walk on eggshells because of its continual disappointed scrutiny and that only by keeping the principles of the "Word of God" can you ever hope to change your behavior. I'm so glad you have rejected that false "god" and embraced Jesus, the Living Word of God who lives in you, as you, and through you, and who facilitates effortless change in you by the power of the Holy Spirit in you! I'm so glad you have embraced the Truth—Jesus! Love, Papa"* ~

Chapter 12

~Doctrine of Poverty~

"If Jesus has been given a name above every name including sickness, poverty and death, and if John was correct in saying that as he is so are you in this world. Then, your name is recognized in the spirit as being above every other name as well."
Don Keathley

We are all filled with every spiritual gift from God, and we can freely give them out to other people, and as we give, we receive for ourselves. It is through his grace and unconditional love that we heal and obtain everything we need to live our life. However, when we are held in bondage by human-made words under religious mindsets, we are captives to poverty. Religion is an absence of a personal relationship with Jesus, who came and demonstrated the Kingdom within us. If you are looking at all the religious people today and envy their supposed material wealth, you are missing the true riches. Jesus can absolutely give you all the wealth in the world, and there is nothing to feel guilty about regarding money. The importance is not in having money. Our true fulfillment is love, peace, and joy in his Spirit, which is all about a relationship. Would you choose all the money in the world over a relationship with your kids? What about your health? We see people in the world around us choose money, yet they are not healthy-minded or stable people. Jesus is calling you into a relationship with him and God your Father. You are all one in union together, and through love, you will have the healthiest life you could possibly have that will fulfill you with great wealth like Solomon, who was the wisest man in the world. Religion is the world's way of being, yet we are not born from our soul and through ourselves, nor are we created in the image of the world. We are the image of our Father, and Christ is our life and our Spirit within, who guides and directs us into all his riches. The curse of the law is threefold; it is poverty, sickness, and death. We know through Scripture that Christ defeated all forms of sickness and death, so we are now empowered through him. In Matthew 9:35, as Jesus passed through various villages, he healed people because, in the Kingdom of God, heaven is within you and there is no sickness. Sickness, disease, poverty, and evil all came into formation through people's mind separation from God, causing them to do things out of selfish greed. Kingdom living is pure and incorruptible, and when you drink of his water you are purified, cleansing your body and life.

The Lord Jesus Christ, in his marvelous empowerment of grace, does an incredible exchange with us by enlightening us with his truth. He takes on our poverty as us in our fallen mindset, and he reveals the truth which then takes us out of the worldly poverty mentality and into spiritual riches you can manifest in your body and on earth. He identifies with us as us and brings in the replacement of full restoration. We read this in 2 Corinthians 8:9, ***"For you know the grace of our Lord Jesus Christ, that though he was rich, yet for your sakes, he became poor, that you through his poverty might become rich*.**" Christ took all our infirmities and sickness upon himself, and then replaces it with his miraculous healing within us. (Matthew 8:17) We can be of excellent cheer as we operate our lives from out of him who has overcome everything for us.

"These things I have spoken to you that in Me you may have peace, in the world you will have tribulation but be of good cheer, I have overcome the world."
John 16:33

We have come out of death, which are the world's standards based on selfish, greedy acts and enter into his incredible riches. The reason we see so much evil in the world is too many people still do not have the revelation of unconditional love within them. The very heart and passion of the Apostle Paul was to get the grace message out to everyone so the world would be free from selfish ambition, attitudes, and evil deeds. When everyone in the world operates from out of his love for them, you will witness peace on earth as our Father intended all along. I believe this is the very reason Paul tells us in Romans 8:22 that the whole earth groans in pain. It's a side-effect of humans who are not walking in unconditional love. There is so much hurt and anger in the world that all of nature is just as disturbed as most of the people on earth. We are here to take dominion of the earth, and if we did this from out of Christ's love within us then we would see a beautiful glowing healthy earth, that would be just as healthy as every human would be.

We have overcome the world just as Jesus did, and we have his very loving power within us if we choose to focus on heaven and bring his will to earth. God is not the creator of evil, poverty, and sickness, and there is no part in God where evil resides. We can either be influenced through our selfish ways or be influenced by God's way that is centered on his love. God does not like evil, just as we don't like it, therefore this is all the more reason to rise up and become a godly influencer of his love and let that love ripple onto every person you meet. If people do not have the revelation of God's unconditional love for them, then when they hurt, they extend that hurt onto other people. Love is the only cure for total mind and body healing, which is why Jesus instructs us to renew our mind to the Kingdom's way of living. As we learn through our relationship with him, our hearts become more like his, and this transforms our minds.

As our hearts are flooded with his love, our bodies respond from out of that great love, and the earth responds, thus leaving no room for any negative adversaries.

Overcoming is not about how well you perform and how well you obey; it's about the overcomer who has done everything as you. We read in 1 John 4:17, ***"As he is so are, we in this world."*** We need to know who Jesus is because you have authority in this life to be as he is in this present world. You are in union with Christ, and he is everything you need to live fully through your time here on earth. You don't have to overcome anything, the only thing required is to rest and enjoy fellowship with Christ. Your transformation comes through that fellowship union together with him. As you sit and rest, reading, talking, and meditating your mind on him, you will hear him, and a transformation takes place. You start to move out of the wrong mindset into a Christ-centered mindset full of Kingdom riches.

Religious thinking believes that following Jesus involves giving up some things we think we might not want to give up. Religion tells us to give up your time, your talent, your finances, your resources, your fun, your enjoyment, and in return it will give you a good life. If I may be so bold, I would say that if you follow the religious laws of what to do and what not to do, you are probably involved in something that is not good and beneficial for you. These people don't want to get to know Jesus and love because they believe they will have to give up a life of cheating to get what they want.

People believe cheating to get things in life works out for the best because they have money and things, and all the stuff they think they need. But Jesus warns us in Matthew 6 to not be like them because your Father knows what you need. He knows what is safe, healthy, and prosperous for you without you having to worry, stress, steal and cheat to get it. All the pressure and anxiety to gain things and look good in front of people will only bring sickness to your mind and body. Nothing is fulfilling in a life mentally separated from God. It will only end in some form of mind destruction, unhealthy living, and financial loss.

Living a life of cheating and lies is deception, causing people to try and fill themselves up with stuff in an effort to fill the deep dark void that is actually crushing them. People are scared to come to him, lest they lose the very thing that is killing them, which is a distorted wrong lifestyle. Let's read what Jesus had to say about this matter in John 10:10. ***"The thief does not come except to steal, and to kill, and to destroy. I have come that they may have life, and that they may have it more abundantly."*** The thief that Jesus is referring to is lying, cheating, stealing, adultery, murder, and every other evil out there today, as Paul speaks about in Galatians 5:19-21. It's a lie pushed on us by religious laws, and it never stops us from doing evil acts. The law enhances people's chances of doing these things because it repeatedly makes you think about the wrong actions until you follow through with doing what you don't want to do. Fear-produced doctrines make people focus on themselves and what they want, along with the pressure to avoid sinful actions. This is in every dimension, a poverty-stricken mindset that can have disastrous results in our lives and the lives of those around us. The abundant life Jesus Christ came to earth to demonstrate for us is fulfilled through his love.

The prosperous life is Christ in you, the hope of glory, and he wants nothing but the very best for you. His desires will become your desires because knowing what you have need of, he wants to give you everything that will be healthy and profitable for you. You will never miss out because he has far more exceedingly abundant pleasures than you can ever imagine. (Ephesians 3:20-21) That is awesome news! Never be afraid to walk up to your Papa dad and talk openly with him about everything, even all the wrong stuff, addictions, lies, cheating, whatever it is you are struggling with. As you continue to focus on him, he is going to direct you out of all those things that are not good for you. He wants you to enjoy a long and happy, fruitful life, even as your soul prospers. (3 John 1:2) He's trying to add to us, not take something from us. Jesus is trying to give you the same things he has, and he has everything! What if he's not asking for all your finances to drain you dry, but he's actually saying, *"Let's take our finances together. Your finances become Mine, and My finances become yours."* That's a good exchange that you can apply to every area of your life.

There is an excellent story in Luke chapter 18 (paraphrased) that reinforces what I am saying to you about how many people don't understand and believe they can live a victorious life in Christ by simply fellowshipping with him. ***"A certain ruler asked Jesus saying good teacher what shall I do to inherit eternal life,"*** that's the question that many ask, ***"Jesus said why do you call me good no one is good but God, you know the commandments Jesus said, don't commit adultery, don't murder, don't steal, don't bear false witness, honor your father and mother."*** The young man came to Jesus from out of a *doing* religious mentality, and in his pride, he came back to Jesus and said, ***"All these things I've kept from my youth."***

What a liar! He didn't keep those from his youth at all! We know this through reading Scripture. In Romans 3:23, it declares that all have fallen short and there is not one person in the world other than Christ who has not sinned. After the rich young ruler said he met all the *doing* requirements, Jesus then proceeded to say, *"Okay, you've met them but now let's see if you want to follow Me or follow yourself.* In Luke 18:22, he said, ***"So when Jesus heard these things, he said to him, You still lack one***

thing. Sell all that you have and distribute to the poor, and you will have treasures in heaven, and come, follow Me."

The rich young ruler told Jesus that he obeyed and had been loyal in doing things for God. However, Jesus explained the Kingdom mentality that God is relational, and we live by trusting and walking with God because he ultimately knows what is right for our individual lives.

So, Jesus asks the young ruler who claimed to have obeyed all the law to go and sell everything he had and then give the proceeds to the poor, and if he did then he would have riches in heaven. Unfortunately, he didn't understand because, like many people today, his focus was on his things and his selfish ambition.

"But when he heard this, he became very sorrowful, for he was very rich." Luke 18:23

He had a choice, either choose the riches of heaven and hearing Christ, or chose earthly treasure, and listen to himself. Heaven is here and now within you, and when you trust and walk by faith in Christ, having a sense of inner peace and knowing that even if you can't see it or understand, there is a reason he is saying to do what you need to do. You have the keys to heaven on earth, which is hearing Christ Spirit within you, therefore you hold all of his power to bind up earthly situations and release heaven everywhere you go.

Only God can see ahead and know what will happen, and the best way for you to move forward. We cannot know what is around the corner with certainty, so God always has your best interest at heart, even when it doesn't seem like it. The rich young ruler would have felt the riches of heaven as he gave all to the poor, and perhaps doing this would have given him less anxiety and provided health benefits if he didn't have so many things. He was rich and a ruler, so he wouldn't have been deprived, even after giving everything to the poor, but he would have significantly helped his fellow humans with the excess he had. Jesus didn't suggest the rich ruler give his money to a ministry, he said go and give it to the poor, and if he did that, then Jesus would have made an exchange with him. The exchange that God makes, whether it's your life or his life, your unrighteous for his righteousness, whatever it is, you always benefit from the exchange. He never takes from you, and when he gives, you get far more back than you gave.

God is a giver, he is not a taker. He was actually telling the young ruler, would you like a checking account, or would you rather have the whole bank? If you give, then more comes back to you, pressed down and shaken and poured into your lap. Jesus would have given him far more than he could have imagined! (Luke 6:38) The works of religion will always keep you tied to things and yourself. Through fear, you think that maybe if I draw near to Christ, I won't be as prestigious, or rich, and have all that my eyes can see. Those with this mindset are under a false assumption that walking in his unconditional love takes away things from them, causing them to have lack. There are many reasons God speaks to us on why we need to do what he asks of us, and we can't always see why. We only need to trust him and move where our inner peace is calling us. Listen to the Spirit as he guides; he will not lead you astray.

"Give, and it will be given to you, good measure, pressed down, shaken together and running over, will be poured into your lap. For with the measure that you use, it will be measure back to you." Luke 6:38

You only gain through his love. This is where your health and joy, along with every desire you could ever dream is for you; in the Kingdom. Jesus is calling you away from religious anxiety, and all the heavy guilts and burdens you were never meant to carry around, and this is the reason so many are sick today. What I am teaching you I know from personal experiences in my own life. This is not about giving you mere inspiring words; this is my heart to your heart. I'm talking directly to the Christ Spirit that's in you. Your world is going to change drastically, and for the remarkably better as you press into his love daily. He was made to be sin for our sin so that we may be righteous with his righteousness. He tasted our death so we could taste his life. He took our poverty and gave us his abundance. He took our shame and gave us his glory. He endured our rejection and gave us his acceptance. He took our old man then put it to death that we might have the new man and we would live as him.

This is your new season of life. Decide with me that you're going to leave all forms of institutional religion. I didn't say you had to leave your church or your friends. I'm suggesting all that is religious in your life, is built on straw. The things that try to hold you down need to go. Exchange the bondage life and embrace his abundant life, and let's break out into nothing but graciousness, his goodness to us.

"Your believing, confessing, receiving or faith does not make any objective Kingdom truth happen. Your subjective awakening and progressive opening of the eyes of your understanding makes the objective manifest in your life. Believing, confessing, receiving or faith can only obtain what grace has already given to you void of your action."

Paul never built on theology, or actions or beliefs. He built on Jesus plus nothing and what Jesus has done for us. Wherever you see grace in the Bible, substitute the word Jesus and it will give you some insight into who Jesus is, which is grace. We couldn't make ourselves saved, sanctified, justified, righteous, and blameless, so it was Jesus who did all of this for you, as you.

He rescued us from the loss that comes from sickness and infirmities, from death and poverty. That being the case, why does all the death, poverty, and sickness still capture us? Many people, even Christians, are still unaware of everything he has provided, and they continue looking and focusing on lack and problems rather than on him, where all the answers to every solution resides. You must get yourself to a position of knowing him and spending time talking with him and letting him reveal all that he has given to you. Focus on good thoughts, despite what you are going through, and then see yourself as he sees you, healed, free from all debt, ties, and bondages. Once you have a deep heartfelt conviction in your heart, you will see yourself possessing it.

Use your imagination to see yourself free from sickness, out of debt, and living the life that you have in your heart; it is possible. Personally, I don't take flu shots because I see myself free from the flu. I'm not suggesting anybody not take the flu vaccine because that is a personal decision between you and Jesus. I've got the visualization along with the revelation that poverty is not part of my life. I hold that picture, and I don't speak poverty, nor do I carry the image around any longer where I wondered if I was going to have enough money to make the rent and the car payment. That bothered me for years because I always held the fear of lack. I had to defeat that thinking, and now I have enough money, and I'm not worried about where I'm going to eat lunch, or if I have enough money to buy anything I need.

The Bible says in Proverbs 23:7, ***"That as he thinks in his heart, so is he."*** Ask yourself honestly, how do you see your life, in poverty or provision? What vision do you hold for yourself in all areas of your life? Scripture says as a man thinks, so you don't have an outward problem, you've got an inward problem. It's religious thinking that has kept many Christians in depression and poverty. If he rescued you from all loss, then why are you still in it? Because people don't believe they are rescued. As you think in your heart, so are you, and what you have today is a direct result of your thoughts. Today you can make a start to think on Christ and enjoy your fellowship, then make new plans based on his truth for your life. Situations may not change overnight, and most often, you didn't create your situation overnight either! So, it may take time to manifest what you now hold in your heart, but it will happen at the appointed time.

What you are thinking first comes from out of your heart, you can't just have a head agreement with anything because believing begins in your heart, not your mind. You need time to meditate on truth and let it really go deep within to see the abundant living, just as Christ sees the victory. Our warfare is not some spiritual demon. It is an old wrong mindset that keeps coming back to haunt us that needs to be overridden with his truth. You make a stand and declare that you will not think wrong negative thoughts that are contrary to God's will. Everything good that comes forth from a heart of love is all God's will, health, family, finances, and career. Think about things that are true that you have, even if it hasn't yet arrived in the mail, so to speak! He will direct your steps. He'll direct you to what you need to do to alleviate the sickness and the poverty, and you will be alive in him where death does not exist. In him, we live eternally.

He says in Galatians 3:14 that we have every spiritual blessing, ***"That the blessings of Abraham might come on the Gentiles in Christ Jesus, that we might receive the promise of the Spirit through faith."*** God promised Abraham that everything he put his hand to he would bless. He said every place Abraham's soul and foot touched, and all the land belonged to him, as it does you. He promised Abraham that he would be his constant guide and protector, and this same promise is for you. You are an heir to the promises of God, just as Abraham was through a relationship that is unique to your life with God. Paul said to the Galatian people that all the blessings they have come through Christ who is in you. It does not come through law keeping.

Throughout the Bible, you will read all kinds of different stories as everyone had a different journey with God, and how he spoke to them regarding their life.

God is directing your life for you through a relationship you have with him, and in that, you will be fully satisfied. It does not include poverty or sickness. It will include all good things through the direction he has for you as an individual. Maybe it is not to own all the land in the world or to be the President or the wealthiest person in the world, or maybe it is. The point being, we are not all alike, we are individually created and made in his image and likeness to live our lives through a loving relationship with him.

"The New Testament is written on paper as given by human writers. The New Covenant is the Father's Word of Love, acceptance and inclusion written on your heart, he that has ears..."

We didn't earn it, but we do merit it. Our co-crucifixion with Christ, our co-resurrection, our ascending to heaven at the right hand of the Father in him merits our being worthy to receive the inheritance. You have an inheritance, and it's to everything God promised Abraham. You're not a beggar, you're not a pilgrim, and you're not a stranger in a foreign land just passing through. There's enough of his blessings for every person in the world, and there is no shortage of supply.

I read something on the internet a while ago that totally astounded me. There's not a problem with supply; God has provided plenty for everyone, the problem lies in distribution and greed. In America alone, every year 133 billion pounds of food are wasted. Think about the 133 billion pounds of food wasted, this is almost 1/3 of the supply gone to waste. There's enough to feed everybody on earth with excess, and God has blessed our fields, blessed our harvest, and blessed whatever we put our hands to. We've been the ones who have messed up the distribution of what God has provided. We were all created to love him, and then we would love each other. If we all would share through love, nobody would lack anything because we would look out for one another.

In Philippians 4:19, it says, ***"My God shall supply all of our need according to his riches in glory by Christ Jesus."*** Has God done that? Absolutely. So what's the problem? The problem is we have not done what Joseph did through love; we have not distributed. We have become greedy and self-seeking and failed to look out for one another. We've not been good stewards over what has been placed in our hands. We've been blessed in every area of life, which is Kingdom living if only humanity would make the choice to hear him within and turn to his right way of living.

People have been influenced by religion and into relying on self. They have left grace and gone into law because they didn't talk to Christ and consider it all. When you start reasoning through what Jesus provided for us, there is absolutely no room left for you to embrace any law or standard to earn God's favor. I don't care what you confess and what you believe, this has nothing to do with what he's given to all of us. So, what is Paul doing? He reasons with the reader through the futility of self-effort, and the futility of performance and law-keeping. He reasons it through the uselessness of doing what grace has freely bestowed and what Jesus has done, so we need to remind ourselves of this because our inclination is to always go back towards performance.

I don't care how long you have followed grace; you need to remind yourself you are not merited by your behavior. There is a progression to this, and in Romans 8:14-18, Paul talks about being led by the Spirit. You should be led more by the Spirit today than at any other time. He talks in verses 17-18 about the fellowship of his sufferings and his desire that we might manifest the glory. This process matures us as it did Paul, who could finally say that his grace is sufficient for me as he came through the maturing process.

We are praying to get rid of stuff and God says, *"I'm trying to show you my grace and strength through that weakness."* When you are in tough situations, Christ within you wants to make that exchange with you, to move out of your mentality and for you to begin thinking on the heavenly realm, which will bring his riches to your situation. We are living here to bring heaven to earth, so God is saying my power is right here now within you, so demonstrate it in all situations. Then just like Paul, you will say that it is no longer I who live, it is Christ who lives in me. (Galatians 2:20) You can't come to that place until he has shown himself strong and able in every situation that you face. Christ wants all people to know him, and to live from out of him and walk in his unconditional love. Paul was the man in that time and season to confront the Judaizers with the power of Christ within. Today, you are the person confronting all kinds of people and situations with his passionate fiery love that will transform the way people think, and then provoke and stir up the Christ Spirit within them. We do not run from situations; we face them head on with his grace and unconditional love. It would be fantastic to just ask God, please take this pain away, the hurts I feel, and the people who are my adversaries. However, God wants them to come to his Kingdom so more people will be released from the prison of hell that has them trapped and who are suffering. Freely you have received from Christ, freely you give, and as you give, you receive. The pain and suffering we feel in our situations is real and it does hurt, however, if we continue pressing into Christ and understand that the hurt we feel perhaps has come from people who don't know his love, it can help us to understand some of the *why's* that we face. Remember, the world was created in his love, and the reason we have sickness and evil is because it has been created through human's minds that are absent from God's love. This is the very reason we want to share his message of love and grace, to help all of humanity come to the realization of Christ within.

Then finally, one day, just as Paul said, I finished my course, I've run my race, and I've kept the faith, we too will say these same words. Paul's teachings to the Galatians is equally as important for us today if we are to become consistent in our faith in him. What creates the inconsistency and lack of faith within us is dwelling on the things that religion has been teaching. Get yourself free, cut the bonds, cut the cords, cut the chains, and begin walking in the manifestation of everything God has for you. Enjoy a final thought from author Gary Gagliardi who interpreted the words of Christ from the original Greek language on his website; https://christswords.com/

"Being feeble?"... responded the Master... "help them."

"What if they are dying?...Dying?... Lift them up!"

"What if they look like they have a skin disease?...Scabby? Clean them!"

"And if they are possessed by demons, out of the minds?...Demons? Toss them out!"

"And how much do we charge for providing these services?"

"The Master and several of his original students laughed at the question."

"Gifts, you all got. Gifts give!" the Master answered simply."

Chapter 13

~Deconstructing Religion~

"Pure grace enables us to renounce legalism – a system of living in which you try to make spiritual progress or gain God's blessing based on what you do…It is a major move but one that will transform your life. Walk away from legalism today and don't look back."
Steve McVey

Deconstructing religious methods is not easy because of the many years we have been taught all the lies about God. Even if you weren't taught lies, you have most likely encountered people with religious beliefs who influenced your thoughts. When we become so institutionalized, it can be difficult to work with his Spirit because we are accustomed to having other people set up rules for us to follow. Once we are free from religious bondage, we often return back because it's all we know, and we fear the unknown. There is safety in knowing where you have been, even if the past has had a negative influence in your life. It is the same reason prisoners return to old thought patterns and behaviors, resulting in their committing the same type of crimes and returning to prison. Their thought system has been ingrained in them to where they can't see another way out, and they are often reluctant to believe in a new positive direction. There is a certain kind of comfort in repeating our actions, even if they lead us down that same dead-end road. We know the outcome, so we find safety in what we have been through rather than trusting God in something positive and good for us. The religious thinking lifestyle assures you that you are doing things right for God, so you believe in God's eye's, he approves of you. However, when you stumble and fall from your own good works, you go into a spirit of condemnation and guilt over those actions. If the heart is not right and walking with God, this will always be the outcome, time and time again. Jesus said to the blind Pharisee's in Matthew 23:26, ***"Blind Pharisee, first cleanse the inside of the cup and dish, that the outside of them may be clean also."*** They had all the outward actions that made them look good to people. They believed they looked great for God, but they didn't realize that the inside of their heart was cold. They had no relationship with God, so the actions they thought were right were actually wrong. They didn't operate out of love, and they never saw people in the light of God. They looked down on all the outcasts and never bothered to help them, and if they found anyone interested in what they did, they would train them up to be just like them; religious and cold.

We seem to think that we need to attain to a certain place of discipline and righteous living to feel acceptable to

God. We set up these false illusions in our mind that we have to do certain things to get right, but there are two problems with this mindset. The first problem is, you'll never be able to be perfect all the time, and the second is you're always going to be adding to your performance list because you will see that what you originally had is not working. When you see it's not working, you double down and add more and try harder and become even more determined. And it becomes this never-ending circle where you continue to add and put more onto yourself.

In Galatians 3:11, Paul says, ***"But that no one is justified by the law in the sight of God is evident, for the just shall live by faith."*** The just are you and me because we all have his Spirit within us, and we live from out of him. We are human beings, not human doings. Jesus' cry from the cross was, it is finished. It is finished, and we don't need to add anything to it with our own finishing touches because you cannot add to perfection! We were taught that it's finished, but it's only effective if we ***do*** our part and if we somehow, by our response, finish what he declared as already being a done deal. We were overwhelmed with the idea that it is actually finished, and we can now rest. We struggle to rest, so we say hang on, believing it's not finished without us finishing it.

In Luke 19:10, Jesus said, ***"For the Son of Man has come to seek and to save that which was lost."*** We've looked at the first part of that verse and said that's totally him, he's come to seek us. He's come to seek everybody, but the last half needs our help. He's very effective in seeking, but he's not so effective at saving without our help, without my confession, my prayer, my belief, my faith, or my acceptance of him. Nowhere in that verse do we see any of these stipulations. This is because he said I came to make a covenant with you, and I've come to seek and to save that which is lost. It doesn't matter what you do or what you say, or your faith, for I have made up my mind what I will do.

If he's made up his mind, then consider it done. There is no indication of his needing our help to accomplish his mission, none. he didn't say, "I need your wisdom, and I need your input, I need your help, I need your acceptance, I need your prayer, I need your faith to accomplish My mission." The Father set his mission, and Jesus agreed to it, then he came and fully accomplished it. Paul explains this to the Galatians, who heard his message of grace while having no spiritual background. People who don't know anything about the gospel and Jesus will grasp the gospel message of his unconditional love with ease. It is only after they enter a church that preaches a mixture message with laws that they begin second guessing what they believe. They think that perhaps I need to do something and then enter the church's contract agreement. However, with God nothing is ever lost, and we can be assured that God is calling each person to enter into a relationship with him without all the extra things we think we need to do to win his love.

"Anytime you introduce fear into a relationship it ceases to be a relationship."

All around the world, people have an idea what the gospel is. They've heard about Jesus, and they've heard about hell. Unfortunately, most people have heard more about hell than the unconditional love of God. I'm glad Paul was able to teach the gospel of grace, but then along came controlling religious people telling us we need to do more, and it's not just grace. The Judaizers said that you have to add more. You need to follow through with your religious church requirements, you need to be circumcised, you need to keep the law, and you need to work at keeping your salvation. So, what is work exactly? How do you know what work is? Let me define work for you in a spiritual context. Work is anything you must ***do*** to have what the Father, through the Son, has directly deposited into your life through the finished work of the cross. If you think that you must ***do*** something to receive or have what he said is already yours, it becomes a work. We are no longer centered on what Christ has done for us. The Judaizers came in behind Paul and put all their own stipulations on what people needed to do to be approved by God.

They said it's good that you heard the gospel and accepted Jesus, but to really be approved by God what you need to do now is be circumcised. The laws are not just the ten commandments, or the 613 laws Moses gave to help the people keep the ten. The people, then and now, tried hard to keep the ten commandments, but because they can't they continually add ever more laws to their list, which is exactly why Moses came up with an additional 613 extra laws to help people keep the first ten laws!

We find all kinds of laws and rule-keeping all around the world today through many churches. We have the Baptist Church, Pentecostal, Charismatic, Nazarene, Church of Christ, and all the various add-ons that have been strapped onto people as requirements to either be saved or stay saved and be approved by God. We even write books on how you should conduct yourself, and in many churches today they have a church manual. This is their own set of rules you must agree to by joining their church. In the church manual, you will find their version of the 613 laws of Moses, everything you need to do for you to be in good order with God and make him happy.

It was all laid out for us, so that becomes the problem. It's a nasty business and the reason the church is so impotent today, for it keeps us running in circles, trying to accomplish and add on and do things. It's a full book of what you can do while you are with them and what you can't do, and you agree to be a perfect person during your time with them. You are there to learn about Christ, and many people are coming into the church who are lost. The last thing they need is a guilt trip strapped on them about what God requires for them to do. When they make an error and step out of line, they are under a tremendous amount of guilt and condemnation. There is no love in that type of set up. Their conditions will always set you up to fall at some point, which will keep you feeling insecure with God.

What I'm establishing into your thinking is there is no partial view with God looking at you. How he sees you every day and all the time is as being perfect in him. It's a total lie that God only loves you when you do things right, and the rest of the time you're on your own. He is the entry of total forgiveness who has been given to you for all eternity, and you are perfect in him. God doesn't half forgive; the Father has put unforgiveness in your rearview mirror, and you never have to look back at it.

Most of us have attended a church where a heavy weight was put on us to serve, and I can tell you that's bondage. You feel driven to do something for Jesus. You initially came into the church to be encouraged in the message and to fellowship with other Christians, and then all of a sudden you feel this overwhelming sense that you need to get a job and to serve, and if you don't you are made to feel guilty.

You don't need to feel guilty because you're not serving in the way the traditional church has instructed you to do.

You are serving Jesus as you walk in him every day. And as you live a normal life, whatever you like to do, you are serving him. You are him wherever you go, and you reflect him in whatever you do; that's serving. he does not drive you; he draws you.

"The Holy Spirit never drives us, the Holy Spirit always leads us, and as he leads us, he gives us the desire to do what he leads us to do."

There is a verse in Scripture that absolutely set me free about this because, as a pastor, I always felt driven to do more and more. I was on a hamster wheel for years, seven days a week, 365 days a year, and I never took a vacation for many years. I felt I could not take time away from all that I was doing, and this is a dangerous position to be in. There's a verse in Scripture that set me free. In Philippians 2:13, Paul says that it is God who works in you both to will and to do for his good pleasure. God puts the desire in you. They are his desires, and you are both in union and working with each other through love. Any work you do can be done with his joy and abiding in his Spirit. It is not a struggle, and you won't be working by the sweat of your brow!

God puts the will in you, and then gives you the ability to do that will. If you are driven to serve, I can assure you that sooner or later, you will find the Christian life to be stale and dry. It just becomes a duty because you feel this indebtedness that is a trait of obligation, and it's the preacher's guilt trip they put on you. Here are some examples that you may of heard in church. *"Now ladies and gentlemen, you know how much Jesus has done for you. He lived for you, he died for you, now after everything he did for you, you ungrateful servant, what are you going to do for him?!"*

That is guilt, and it will seep into your heart over time until you become ingrained with having to work for Jesus, and if you don't, then all that guilt will take up residence in you and wreak havoc in your life. It is this religious mindset of all the things you must continually do to be right in God's eyes that will burn you out in the end. I understand this because I was driven to always work for God and myself to be acceptable in his eyes.

Pastors are famous for decorating up words in a way that pulls you in to get you to do something. We know how to be influential in what we want from people. You cheapen God's love for you by thinking you owe him big-time and that you have some kind of duty to pay. The only responsibility you have is to believe how much he loves and cares for you, just as you are.

Your life is not about loving him, serving him, and showing him how diligent you are. It's coming to a place of rest in his love and his care for you to know the riches of his grace. It then becomes an effortless response to move in all he has for you from out of him, and it's no longer exhausting because you are at rest in him.

Grace never obligates you or puts you under a guilt trip and love never demands. Love shows and demonstrates, and from out of that love you will naturally respond in love.

Paul tapped into a source that enabled him to go past this place of burnout. Can you go seven days a week? I think you can. If you learn how to rest in him, you can take a vacation all the time because you are not working out of your soul, you're not working out of your emotions, you're not working out of your own drive. I've learned that when I get cranky and arrive at that hard-working place within my soul, it's because I have been making all the effort, and I need to back off.

Paul learned that there is a place where we rest, yet we never cease from working with him. In 2 Corinthians 5:14, Paul says, ***"For the love of Christ compels us."*** It's not an obligation that draws us to try and balance the scales because we think we need to now do something for him. It is living your life from what he has done for you. All you are doing is putting your mind and focus on him, tuning your ears into his Spirit, and you then flow each day from him.

It's a divine privilege and a delight, for his love compels us because we judge that if One died for all, then all died. We love him because he first loved us, and all we are doing is responding from out of his love. (1 John 4:19) We are not trying to do something for him to invoke his favor towards us. This is the motivation when we have an attitude of religion, and maybe some of that is still stuck on you. You still feel a little bit bad, like you're not doing enough. I've come into this grace message, I'm not doing anything for Jesus, you reason. Yes, you are! Your whole life is in him now, and in everything you do you are serving and demonstrating him through love. You now understand that even though you don't have to live for him, he's living as you. He's not even living through you; he's living as you and there is a total union between the two of you. When you live your life in the Spirit and move through everything you do through love, you will continue to bear fruit. By meditating on him and in Scripture through the eyes of love, you will be transformed from bondage to freedom. It might happen overnight, or it might take some time. Just keep walking with him because he will put the light on your path and direct you straight into the liberty of his perfect love that will ultimately set you completely free.

We serve by appearances, but we know that we are sons by position; that's the mentality. So, if you feel like, *"Well, I know that I'm a servant of the Lord, I'm just here to serve God,"* that's the mentality. Your spirit is one with his Spirit, so the only thing to do is line up your thinking and thoughts onto him. If you are constantly thinking and meditating on Christ, how will you have time for your thoughts to drift into other areas that are consumed with negativity and works? You won't have the time. You will be transformed from the renewing of your mind, and then you know what is good, and acceptable, and true, as you naturally live from out of your spirit union with Him, and not through soul direction.

"When Christ who is our life appears, then you also will appear with Him in glory." Colossians 3:4

Living your life from out of works, negativity, slaving away in wrong beliefs and demands are an Old Testament mentality. In the Old Covenant, there were no sons of God. Jesus was the firstborn among many brethren. There were no sons of God walking the earth like you and me today. They had an uncertainty of position that produced a rational response to perform. However, that performance could never be enough, and those under the Old Covenant suffered from a lot of performance anxiety, and that's what burned Israel out so often. Israel as a nation lived in the obedience of God, then they fell off before returning to obedience and then fell off again, and they repented. The nation of Israel revolved around performance anxiety, and they couldn't be obedient long enough. They were not strong enough to achieve what they felt they needed to do if they wanted to receive the blessings from God. It's like a treadmill where you can't seem to get off, eventually you're exhausted and give up! There is a better way to live healthy than being on a treadmill continually!

What do you think motivated Moses to take the ten Commandments? Five were interpersonal relationships from human to human, and the rest were relationships governing a person's relationship to God. Five were parallel, and five were horizontal. Why did Moses take those Ten Commandments and stretch them out to 613? It was for a performance that produced anxiety, and it was trusting in the observance of all the do's and do not's that they thought would please God. Remember the Sabbath day that was to be kept holy? This was one of the commands, but Moses developed all these subsets to keep the Sabbath day holy. You can't walk too far, you can't do any labor, and you can't make an animal work.

You develop a whole lot of rules and laws to try to enforce the observance of performance, but the problem is, the more laws you develop, the farther you are from obeying the original law until you can't even obey the subset! What do you think created all the laws of the Catholic church, the Baptist church, or the Pentecostal church? They all have their own peculiar set of laws, but why did they do this? They did not see the Father's reflection in Jesus; instead, they saw an Old Testament God who was angry, judgmental, and punitive, demanding absolute obedience.

Remember what religion means? *It is an obligation by humans to their God in return for peace, blessings, and prosperity.* Religious laws still drive people to this day. It's what drove Moses to go from ten to 613, and in churches today what do they tell us to do if we are not living in peace, blessings, and the prosperity we want?

They teach us to double down on what we have been doing. Double down on your giving, double down on your obedience, and your commitment to him. Try harder to do what failed to work the first time, they tell us. That's a formula for insanity—trying harder to produce what you couldn't do with a set of rules by adding on more rules. Maybe that's why Paul said in Romans chapter 8, you have not received the Spirit of bondage again to fear, but you have received the Spirit of adoption by which you cry daddy, Abba - Father.

Your Papa Father knows you need to only hear him for everything pertaining to your life. There is no church manual, pastor, or a prophet who can hear God for your life. They can give you advice and guide you with some wisdom, but ultimately it is through God speaking to you personally that you will receive all his blessings. As you press into him, you will be transformed through an effortless process, and what you will then discover is all those things you thought you needed to make your life such a blessing was already in you. You will find that it was never found in things. True fulfillment is only found in him, the person who is Christ's unconditional love and grace, who brings you all the peace and joy. When you realize his love, you will know that you have everything in life, now and eternally. I encourage you today to press into your passionate love union that is an individual relationship you have with Christ. Hear Him personally for your life as He reveals His true riches in your heart. As you hear Him you will transform and move into the life that He always designed for you in His complete loving abundance.

I would like to share with you an inspiring reading from author Mo Thomas documenting his incredible encounter with God's love in his book, *"Into the Abyss: Discover Your True Identity in the Infinite Depths of Christ."* God's unfailing and intoxicating passionate love transformed Mo's religious view. Here is a reading from his beautiful mystical book.

~ "At some point along our journey, some of us who grew up in a religious tradition start questioning our long-held beliefs. Sometimes, these questions lead us down pathways that are unfamiliar to our minds and hearts. This is perfectly normal, and God loves our authentic questions. In fact, I'm not sure that true growth can take place without them. At times however, this process can be frustrating, frightening, and fiercely confrontational. Perhaps our questions are offensive to friends and family members

who now see us as careless heretics, because they perceive our doubts and questions to be dangerous. It might feel like we're losing our foundation, and that all we've known has become uncertain. Our souls may experience the unbearable weight of loneliness as we go through the process of faith-deconstruction.

I do know for certain, and have become fully persuaded, that God is pure Love, and everything else we know about Their character aligns with this love. My internal portraits of God have become far more beautiful as a result, though I'm well aware that "God" exists light years beyond my/our most eloquent concepts about God." ~

Chapter 14

~Grace Plus Nothing~

"If you tell me that I teach a cheap grace, I will tell you that you are still charging too much for grace. Grace is not cheap it's free."
Don Keathley

In this final chapter I will summarize and highlight the essential key points that it is only by entering into a relationship with Christ through grace and unconditional love that effortless change and freedom is possible. We have covered a number of topics regarding religious bondage through this book that perhaps were hidden within you until now. Your life is an individual journey with Christ that you walk out daily as he reveals truths to you. I want to encourage you to pursue and intentionally focus on his never-ending passionate unconditional love, so you can lead a rich and healthy life. If you allow yourself to think about him and receive his living word into your heart, there will be no stopping the divine treasures for your life. Now is the time to dismantle the myths and put your trust in his grace and unconditional love, who is the person of Christ Jesus.

Religion sold you a lie and poisoned your mind, but not any longer. You have the choice to change how you think through the empowerment of Christ in you and to discover your rightful true inheritance that you have in Christ. Religion demanded things not even the teachers of the law could keep, sabotaging your opportunity to live a prosperous life as God intended. You are deceived if you continue to lead a religious life like the Judaizers of Paul's day. Grace is the answer, and is the solution, you live by faith in the Son of God. (Galatians 2:20) He calls all people to have a relationship with Him in unconditional love.

There is nothing in anything Paul taught that requires us to do any outward religious works to please God. I will encourage you with some insight into what Paul said. It was his mission to show the Gentiles and everyone he encountered God's loving character, and the very person of grace himself. Paul, speaking to us in 1 Corinthians 1:26, explains that grace is for everyone, but not many mighty are called or those who are noble. Most of the time, it is oppressed people who turn to Christ. They want to change their lives, so they start to look outside of everything they have ever been taught and begin to ask God questions and reach out to him. God has chosen the foolish things of this world to shame the wise, and he has chosen the weak things of the world to put to shame the mighty things. Nobody can get the credit for what God has done, which is exactly what religious people attempt to do. They rely on their own knowledge and self-performance rather than praising God and rely on hearing him for their lives. He has made you in Christ Jesus, righteous, and sanctified in him regardless of your choices.

When you make poor decisions, and everyone does, you will find that religion is quick to kick you to the curb and point the finger. There are plenty of us who have made mistakes, and there is nobody who hasn't. Jesus was the only perfect human because he only did what he saw the Father doing. Jesus learned obedience through the things that he suffered. I want to reassure you today that grace and the unconditional love of God are for you, no matter what you've thought or done in life. We can read a lot of encouraging stories through the Bible from godly people who had all kinds of challenges, yet they overcame all things with God.

Let's look at the life of Moses. He missed it greatly with his terrible choice to kill an Egyptian and then flee to the hillside, yet God brought him back from out of his own fears. (Exodus 2:11-15) We must rest, trust, and believe; if we don't, it will lead us to make poor choices. In the life of Jonah, he went directly against God's calling for his life. He didn't want to listen to God and demonstrate his love for the people at Nineveh. Instead, Jonah wanted them to suffer but that's not God's heart. Jonah knew if he went to Nineveh and did what God asked, the people would repent and be forgiven. In the early stages of God calling Jonah, he didn't want the people to be forgiven. He was acting out of his own cold heart until God reached him and directed him accordingly through his loving persuasion.

We read in 1 Samuel 22, how David assembled the greatest military fighting machine on the planet in his time, and they were an unbeatable force. They were a unique army, and David was on the run, but God was working in his life. Yet David hit a low point time after time, during which he must have felt like a loser before God. David escaped and went to the cave of Adullam, but God's army was dissatisfied and felt lost. However, God told David that he was a man after his own heart, and this is what God is saying about you today. You are after God's own heart, and this is the reason you are worried and try in your own strength, because you want to please him.

Today God is establishing a grace army, and you are the image and likeness of God as unveiled in the likeness of Jesus. He is using every person, even religious people who have been shunned by the church. Religion doesn't want to know anything about who you are or what you are facing. It is all about rules, not love. You don't need to feel labeled by the church or have your situations dictate who you are. Wherever you are today, you can think about God and meditate on his love for you. There are times in our life that we are down, but not out. God is in you, and he is relentlessly pursuing you with his passion. Even if you purposely go into another direction from where God called you, he will redirect you just like a GPS! You may go around the long way and through a lot of traffic, but eventually you will listen, and your heart will change.

"God created the earth and everything in it, but humans created the world and everything in it."

God is going to lift you higher than ever before, and you will see his unfailing love that he has for all people, no matter what they have done in life. It is never too late. Don't be discouraged, don't be perplexed, don't be feeling abused; this is your time to grow and learn in grace. His grace expresses to us that even though we are pressed on every side, we are not crushed. We will not despair, and although we may have been persecuted, we are not forsaken. His love will prevail. During those time we feel struck down, his mercy will overpower us, and we will not be destroyed. All the misery you are feeling resides within the soul realm and is of the world. Its desires are pointless, and they have no life in them. It is the dying of the Lord Jesus Christ, yet he rose and has the victory, and he will manifest himself in your body. This is the very journey God has taken you on so you will experience his love and mercy for yourself, and then go on to restore other religious people and anyone who is trapped in deception.

After reading this book, I want you to feel empowered in the Spirit and pursue his truths, because this is your life with him, and God only has love, peace, and joy for you.

There will be times that are hard in life and will cause you to be upset, however, the rest comes when you take what is happening to God and allow him to minister peace to you. When Paul was at the pinnacle of his religious leadership, he persecuted the church, killed believers, imprisoned men, women, and children because they followed Jesus. Suddenly, Paul had an encounter with Jesus with his unconditional love and mercy, and he was sent out to strengthen those same ones he persecuted. Paul transformed, and God empowered him to reach countless people to know the love and grace of God.

During his ministry he had numerous trials that would be enough to shatter anyone of us. But he was not traumatized because he remained in Christ's love, and that love directed him and brought him peace through everything the world tried to do to him. Paul had to work through a lot of worldly baggage that was not the truth, and I'm pretty sure that's why he spent so many years in the desert working through everything with God, until he saw life through his eyes. And we too may need some time out, and time alone in our own desert where nothing seems to be happening. It's just barren, but then one day we are strengthened, knowing we have worked through it all with God, and we now see the truth. The very gates of all your adversaries, which is your own personal hell and trauma, will not stop grace and God's passionate, unconditional love for you.

"However, when he, the Spirit of truth, has come, He will guide you into all truths, for he will not speak on his own authority, but whatever he hears he will speak, and he will tell you things to come."
John 16:13

Divinity has placed you right where you are for such a time as this, and it is now your time to metanoia, which is to change your mind. Accept God's grace, and don't listen to the voice trying to bring you back to where you were in the land of bondage. No divorce, no prison, and nothing you have done will stop the unconditional love of God.

We tend to have these soulish inclinations that try to pull us back into doing something to merit what has come to us by grace, so this is an easy area where people can influence our minds if we allow them to. You have never missed it with God, and Jesus never looked at any person other than through the eyes of his unconditional love. Often, when we are at a low point many of us wake up and begin to discover that we are in the very center of his will. His strength is made perfect in our weakness. Paul said no flesh could glory in his presence, and when we come to the end of our strength, it is then his strength which is perfected in our weakness.

Paul had a boldness that we should all be aiming for, and that is to know him through the eyes of grace and everything he has already done for us. Paul never backed down from God's love, instead he moved right away from religion. Paul said in Galatians 1:8 that if anybody, including an angel, comes and preaches to you something that I didn't preach to you, then let him be accursed. That is boldness! The key to Paul's boldness and confidence was knowing that his revelation was given to him directly by Jesus. Paul was not concerned with pleasing men; he was only interested in reaching people with the truth that Christ revealed to him for all the Gentiles.

To please people who are living for the world's pleasures it is not difficult. You can follow the easy way and jump on board with any mixture of message out there. However, once you have Christ's grace and love within you and your eyes are opened, it would be impossible to step into all of that and try to go on pleasing people. Your heart becomes Christ's heart, and his passion is your passion, so you can't help but share his love for all people once you break away from the veil of religion.

The church, who are you and me, are his body, and the body is the fullness of Christ. Jesus was the human man, and Christ was the eternal Spirit. I am Don, the flesh man, and Christ is the eternal Spirit that resides within me. I could be called Don Christ, and you may be Billy Christ, Suzie Christ, or whatever your first name is. You are the fullness of him, who fills all and is in all people.

Jesus is the author and finisher of our faith, as we read in Hebrews 12:2. And if he's the author and the finisher, then he's also everything in between. When you hear a distorted gospel, they will emphasize methodology, formulas, laws, and rules which denominations exalt above the person of Christ and his finished work. We've seen a tremendous distortion through platform stars, and we want to be like the guy on the television and at the conferences. So, we create all these filters and add the person's personal ideas and the message they are giving so we can become like them, and in doing so, we take our eyes of Jesus.

We do not need to be like any person, we are all created unique with our own talents and gifts, and above all, we follow Christ, not people. We may hear a great message, and the Spirit of Truth will light up and reveal truths previously hidden until the time we are ready to receive the message, but it's all to reveal Christ in you.

We need to be aiming straight ahead to the bullseye, just as Paul said in Philippians 3:14. ***"I press towards the goal for the prize of the upward call of God in Christ Jesus."*** There's one prize, and it's in Christ, who is not a denomination or a building. He is alive and active in you, where you get to hear him directly for yourself any moment you like. The prophets of the Old Testament were speaking on behalf of God. They were the mouthpiece for God concerning things, however, when Jesus resurrected, his Spirit entered all humans from past generations that had passed away to all the people in that day, and all those who are yet to be born. Every person ever on the earth has the living Spirit of Christ in them. They just need to realize this, and they will be transformed. We can receive encouragement from all people in the body of Christ in any area that they operate in, however, it is you hearing God for yourself that will ultimately change your life.

We can frustrate God's grace when we try to produce knowledge ourselves by leaving the Spirit of Truth out. In John 3:30, John the Baptist said that, ***"He must increase, but I must decrease."*** He is the One who becomes greater, and you are the person who rests in all he has done for you. You don't need to increase to prove yourself worthy through your ability to perform for him, you are worthy every day, just as you are. He will increase in you as you press into Christ, and the more you become aware of his unconditional love for you, the more you will naturally flow from him, and then he increases, and you will decrease.

"Be of good courage. You may be led by the Spirit into the wilderness, but you will come out in the power of the Spirit."

The way to move away from religious works and laws is to intentionally focus your mind on Christ and talk to him daily about all of your life, the good and the bad. Sit at his feet just like Martha did and soak in his love for you. Read and meditate, think on the Scriptures, and ask him to show you the truth. Put your focus on his great love for you, and soak into your relationship with Him. When you sit with him long enough, you will start seeing his love in all areas of your life, and as you see him and your heart shifts to his heart, and you will conduct your life from out of him naturally. You will respond from out of how he speaks to you through love, not through guilt, works, and judgments. That is not who he is at all. He has delivered you and saved you, and you will not miss the mark, for you have the stamp of his authentic identity.

Be of good cheer, even if you have only just begun your journey in grace, because Jesus recognizes and understands that people have limits as to what they're able to embrace at any given time. Jesus informs us in John 16:12 that he had a lot of things to say, but some people could not bear his message *now*. That word *now* is important to note because he never said they would never understand his message. It was at that particular time in their life that they could not bear it, but the time will come when they can receive the message he is speaking to them, just as it is for us today. There are many reasons that, perhaps until now, you could not hear what Christ within was saying, but today, if you choose to you can hear him and rejoice.

As we conclude, I want to share my final thought with you, and for you to know I love and care for you. It is my very heart speaking to your heart to teach you truths that will set you on the pathway to freedom.

Every moment, you get to have your own personal one on one time with Christ in you, who is ready to teach you all things when you are in the position to receive them. Take heart if you feel like you've made a mess of your life and can't seem to please God no matter what you do, so you feel like there's no point in even trying anymore. Always remember, you can't miss the will of God. It may feel like every time you try that everything goes against you, and you might feel unworthy or that you missed it, but you haven't. Those false feelings are the results of years that you soaked into religion.

There is a light at the end of that very dark tunnel, and you are more than a conqueror in him. I want you to know that every hurt has been washing away and all that remains is pure unconditional love for you. There is nothing to be ashamed of due to the poor decisions and choices you made when you were held under religious bondage. You went on what you knew at the time, but now you know and understand a better way, Christ's way; and it's time to lay hold of what is ahead and not go back into holding yourself in captivity. Perhaps you are currently in situations you would rather not be in as you walk with God through grace. Rest assured, wherever you are he is there with you. There are times in our life where our situations can feel uncomfortable because those around us are not walking in the grace of God. Times of sacrifice are needed to help people see the unconditional love and truths of God. Like you, they need mental freedom from the illogical life they are living. Maybe you are living with a religious person who just can't see grace and the finished work of the cross, or perhaps you are suffering due to your own misconduct but now you know better. There are many situations a lot of people pray to be free from and head over to where the grass is greener on the other side. However, when you know Christ within, he becomes your mental strength, your peace, your freedom, and your joy even through life's hardest challenges. He will direct you to where you need to be, he has not ever left you.

Through everything you learn, your mess will go on to become your message of triumph from what God has pulled you through. There is a season for everything in life, and sacrificing your own comfort to help those who need Christ is the noblest thing you can ever do for your fellow human beings. You never need to feel ashamed for being who you are in Christ and standing for righteousness in all situations. The characteristic of healing people and setting them free is often overlooked in religion and the Christian mixed messages that encourage pleasures by sight and good feelings rather than the true riches that come from knowing Christ in your own personal relationship. We all want to enjoy heaven on earth now, and we can, but not everyone knows we can, and it is being a witness, which is you being you, in Christ and demonstrating him naturally to the lost, and healing the sick and the downcast to be mentally restored. You have a choice, and it will always be a choice to hear love or fear. When you remove hearing fear within it takes the anxiety and stress with it, enabling you to hear God a lot clearer, like fine tuning a radio to eliminate the static. Then you are far more empowered to hear and be inspired with what he puts on your heart. He is always for you and never against you.

The gauge for you to know whether you are in religion or grace is simple. We find the answer in 1 John 4:18 where we read; ***"Perfect love will cast out all fear."*** When you know his absolute perfect, unconditional love for you and are immersed in him as he is in you, no fear will reside in you. Meditate on him, soak in his love, set your mind on him, and gaze your eyes on his perfect freedom of love. Paul's message is for us all today, and every part of his teaching is based on God's love that will ask nothing of you. All love wants to do is love you and for you to respond from out of his love in everything you do. There is only grace plus nothing else added, and it is as simple as changing your wrong thoughts in exchange for the mind of Christ, who is within you. You can know the right way for your life and what the outcome will be. Your success is assured when everything you do comes from a position of love because, ***"Love never fails."*** (1 Corinthians 13:8)

And finally, brethren, I want to pray for you. This prayer is taken from one of my favorite Scriptures in Ephesians 1:18-21.

~ I pray that God will give you the wisdom and illuminate the eyes of your understanding to know what is the hope and the ultimate riches of his calling to you, his beloved saint, that you will know the depth of his inheritance that you have in him, with all exceeding abundance, and his dunamis power, strength and might, the very essence and eternal authority that raised Jesus from the dead is known to you who has his supremacy here on earth just as it is in heaven. I pray that you encounter his all-consuming fire of unconditional love and his light that will flood your heart to know what is his calling and all the true wealth of God's indestructible magnificence, Christ in you the hope of glory.~

God Bless you

Don Keathley

Endnotes

For additional inspired reading resources, in no particular order:

Don Keathley; Hell's Illusion
https://www.amazon.com/dp/B08DF828H2/ref=mp_s_a_1_1?dchild=1&keywords=hells+illusion&qid=1595456486&sr=8-1

Paul Gray, *#1 Amazon Best-Selling Author of Convertible Conversations*
Grace Community Facilitator — helping each other experience *Real Life! Host of "Grace to All" Podcast at:*
https://omny.fm/shows/grace-to-all
Notes From Papa
The Fish Net Experience
Grace Is

Steve McVey
Grace Walk Moments
Beyond an Angry God

Baxter Kruger
Patmos

Don Keathley

The Shack Revisited

Parable of the Dancing God

Ralph Harris *God's Astounding Opinion of You*

William Paul Young *The Shack*

Jeff Turner *Saints in the Arms of a Happy God*

Francois Du Toit *Mirror Bible Paraphrase*

Richard Rohr *The Divine Dance*

Andre Rabe

Adventures in Christ

The Secret of Contentment

Metanoia

Desire

Imagine

Blaise Foret *It is Finished*

John Crowder

Cosmos Reborn

Mystical Union

Roy Richmond

Simple Answers to What Seem to be Difficult Questions

George. W. Sarris *heavens Doors*

George MacDonald *The Unspoken Sermons*

Wm. Paul Young

Religion Busters

Cross Roads

Lies We Believe About God

Brian D. McLaren *We Make the Road By Walking*

Dan Stone & Greg Smith *The Rest of the Gospel*

Preston Gillham

No Mercy

Battle for the Round Tower

Steve McVey & Mike Quarles

Helping Others Overcome Addiction

Tullian Tchividjian *One Way Love*

Mike Miller *Been There, Done That*

Thomas Talbott *The Inescapable Love of God*

Bradly Jersak

A More Christlike God

Here Gates Will Never Be Shut

Ivan A. Rogers

No Penal Substitution Parts 1 and 2

Devotional Books

Charles Slagle *Abba Calling*

George MacDonald *Consuming Fire*

Oswald Chambers *My Utmost for his Highest*

Recommended Grace Websites:

https://perichoresis.org/
http://www.gracewalk.org/
http://www.donkeathley.org/
https://gracewithpaulgray.com/
https://www.godnoreligion.com/

Contact Page

Author: Don Keathley
http://www.donkeathley.com/
jdnzf@msn.com

Natasha Trezebiatowski:
Inspired writer, transcriber
https://www.godnoreligion.com/
godnoreligion.god@gmail.com